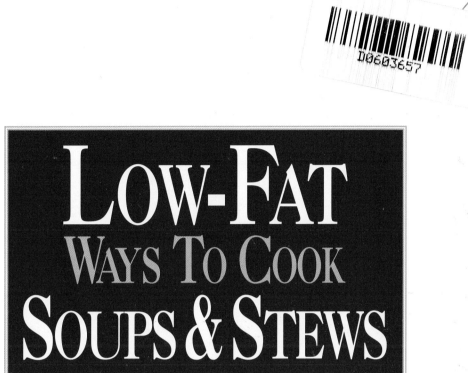

LOW-FAT
WAYS TO COOK
SOUPS & STEWS

LOW-FAT
WAYS TO COOK
SOUPS & STEWS

COMPILED AND EDITED BY
SUSAN M. MCINTOSH, M.S., R.D.

Oxmoor
House®

Library of Congress Catalog Number: 96-71085
ISBN: 0-8487-2214-0
Manufactured in the United States of America
First Printing 1997

Editor-in-Chief: Nancy Fitzpatrick Wyatt
Editorial Director, Special Interest Publications: Ann H. Harvey
Senior Foods Editor: Katherine M. Eakin
Senior Editor, Editorial Services: Olivia Kindig Wells
Art Director: James Boone

Low-Fat Ways To Cook Soups & Stews

Menu and Recipe Consultant: Susan McEwen McIntosh, M.S., R.D.
Assistant Editor: Kelly Hooper Troiano
Associate Foods Editor: Anne Chappell Cain, M.S., M.P.H., R.D.
Copy Editor: Shari K. Wimberly
Editorial Assistant: Kaye Howard Smith
Indexer: Mary Ann Laurens
Associate Art Director: Cynthia R. Cooper
Designer: Carol Damsky
Senior Photographer: Jim Bathie
Photographers: Howard L. Puckett, *Cooking Light* magazine;
 Ralph Anderson, Brit Huckabay; Rita Maas (page 77)
Senior Photo Stylist: Kay E. Clarke
Photo Stylists: Cindy Manning Barr, *Cooking Light* magazine;
 Virginia R. Cravens
Production and Distribution Director: Phillip Lee
Associate Production Manager: Vanessa Cobbs Richardson
Production Assistant: Faye Porter Bonner

We're Here for You!

We at Oxmoor House are dedi-
cated to serving you with reliable
information that expands your
imagination and enriches your life.
We welcome your comments and
suggestions. Please write to us at:

Oxmoor House, Inc.
Editor, *Low-Fat Ways
 To Cook Soups & Stews*
2100 Lakeshore Drive
Birmingham, AL 35209

Our appreciation to the staff of *Cooking Light* magazine and to the Southern
Progress Corporation library staff for their contributions to this book.

Cover: *Jamaican Chili (recipe on page 125)*
Frontispiece: *Vegetable-Barley Soup (recipe on page 120)*

CONTENTS

Soup's On!

*S*oup is comfort food at its best! Heartwarming and satisfying, a good soup, according to many mothers, will "stick-to-your-ribs." Versatile soups and stews have long been acknowledged as a source of nourishment and now, in this book, they have the added health bonus of being low in fat.

Nothing can be quite as nutritious as a simple bowl of soup. Often loaded with vitamin-rich vegetables, soups can provide valuable fiber and complex carbohydrates. Grains and legumes also boost the nutrient values of soups and stews. And many of these contain enough protein to be considered one-dish meals.

These attributes make soups and stews well-suited to today's busy lifestyle. In many cases, all you need to do is add bread and perhaps a salad and you have a complete meal. Also, most soups and stews taste even better when refrigerated a day or so. The flavors blend and intensify, making soups and stews excellent choices for make-ahead meals. Turn to the Sensible Dinners section that begins on page 13 for specific suggestions on creating meals built around soups.

In addition to nutrient value and convenience, soups and stews offer a quick solution to low-fat cooking, as their fat grams can be kept below 30 percent of total calories without extra effort. The over 150 recipes in *Low-Fat Ways To Cook Soups and Stews* show you how it's done.

Start with the refreshing cold soups that serve as appetizers or desserts but do not have a heavy cream base. Next, you'll find hearty dishes made with meat, fish, or poultry. An entire chapter is devoted to soups and stews that feature vegetables. The book concludes with an assortment of satisfying recipes for chilies, chowders, gumbos, and ragoûts.

Before you get started, here's a guide to recommended equipment and techniques for preparing soups and stews the low-fat way.

Kitchen Equipment

The first three items listed are invaluable pieces of equipment for soup-making. Also included are tools designed to help with low-fat food preparation.

• **Dutch oven** or **stockpot**. A Dutch oven should be large enough to accommodate several quarts of liquid. You will want it to have a tight-fitting lid and a flat bottom for best contact with the heat source. Handles should be strong enough to support the weight of the pan when filled.

A Dutch oven or stockpot is best for soup-making.

• **Electric blender.** Use the blender to puree ingredients for thickening cream soups. Allow hot mixtures to cool slightly before pureeing.

• **Food processor.** Use a processor to puree as well as chop the many vegetables that are used in soup-making. The mini-chopper is good for small quantities of fresh herbs or garlic.

• **Colander**. A colander or strainer allows you to drain fat from cooked ground meats.

• **Cutting utensils**. A good-quality knife and cutting board are essential for cutting vegetables, meat, poultry, and fish.

• **Fat skimmer**. Use this specialty item to skim fat from soups, stews, and stocks. Let the soup stand for a few minutes to allow the fat to rise to the top before using the skimmer.

Remove fat with a fat skimmer.

• **Gravy strainer**. A cup with a spout at the bottom is useful to defat broths or thin soups. Pour broth into the strainer, allow the fat to rise to the top, and strain the low-fat broth through the spout.

Use a gravy strainer to defat broth.

• **Measuring cups**. Dry and liquid measuring cups are helpful in preparing and serving soups and stews.

• **Scales**. Food scales assist you in determining correct ingredient amounts and portion sizes. (See page 10 for tips on menu planning and serving sizes.)

FAT TRIMMERS

These techniques are effective when it comes to making a low-fat soup or stew:

• Choose lean meats, poultry, and fish, and trim excess fat before cooking.

• Coat the Dutch oven or stockpot with cooking spray instead of adding oil before sautéing vegetables or meat.

• Brown ground meat, turkey, or chicken in a Dutch oven coated with cooking spray. After cooking, spoon the cooked ground meat into a colander to drain excess fat.

• Pat meat dry with paper towels after draining to further reduce the fat content of cooked ground meat. If other ingredients are to be added back to the pan, wipe drippings from pan with a paper towel.

• Use reduced-fat dairy products such as skim milk, evaporated skimmed milk, and reduced-fat or nonfat yogurt, cheese, and sour cream.

• Cook with wines and other spirits to add flavor but no fat. Most of the alcohol and calories will evaporate during cooking, leaving only the flavor behind.

• A quick way to defat soups, stews, and broths is to let the mixture cool slightly, and then add several ice cubes to the warm liquid. The fat will cling to the ice cubes, which can then be removed and discarded.

Add ice cubes to soup to remove fat.

• If you have time, make soups, stews, and stocks or broths the day before serving, and chill overnight in the refrigerator. After the soup has chilled, skim off the hardened fat with a spoon, discard the fat, and then reheat.

BROTH MADE FROM SCRATCH

*T*o keep soups and stews low in fat, start with a fat-free broth or stock. Although canned broth is fine, you may find that homemade broth yields the best flavor.

• Homemade broths may require a long time for simmering, but they don't require much work. It's not even necessary to peel or trim the vegetables because they will be strained out after cooking. Just wash them thoroughly before starting.

• To produce a more flavorful stock, cut all vegetables into pieces, remove excess fat from bones, and crack large bones.

• To achieve a clear stock, carefully skim the foam from the surface of the mixture as it rises during cooking.

• It is best to simmer the stock gently throughout the cooking time. Avoid rapid boiling.

• When the cooking time is completed, strain the broth through several thicknesses of cheesecloth to remove meat, vegetables, and small particles. Allow the broth to cool thoroughly so that the fat can rise to the surface and be removed.

• The most effective way to remove fat from cooked broth is to chill it—during chilling, the fat rises to the top and hardens. Then it's easy to lift and discard the solidified fat. You can also use a fat skimmer or gravy strainer as described on page 7 to remove unwanted fat.

Skim hardened fat from chilled broth.

Here are four basic broths and stocks that can be used in recipes calling for canned broths.

BEEF BROTH

4 pounds cut-up beef shanks
12 cups water
3 stalks celery with leaves, cut into 1-inch pieces
2 carrots, scraped and cut into 1-inch pieces
2 medium onions, quartered
3 cloves garlic
2 bay leaves
¾ teaspoon salt
¾ teaspoon pepper

Place beef shanks in a 13- x 9- x 2-inch pan; bake at 400° for 20 to 25 minutes or until beef shanks are browned.

Place browned beef shanks and drippings in a large Dutch oven; add water and remaining ingredients. Bring mixture to a boil; cover, reduce heat, and simmer 2 hours. Strain broth through a cheesecloth- or paper towel-lined sieve. Reserve beef shanks and vegetables for other uses; discard bay leaves. Cover and chill. Yield: 12 (1-cup) servings.

PER SERVING: 22 CALORIES (0% FROM FAT)
FAT 0.0G (SATURATED FAT 0.0G)
PROTEIN 0.5G   CARBOHYDRATE 2.0G
CHOLESTEROL 0MG   SODIUM 154MG

Canned Broths

The recipes in this book call for a variety of canned broths. You will see terms such as "no-salt-added," "low-sodium," "low-salt," and "fat-free," depending on what was used in testing. If you are unable to find the broth listed, substitute an equal amount of another type (canned or homemade), but realize that the soup may taste more or less salty if you do. Adjust the salt before serving.

Bouillon cubes, granules, and powdered mixes diluted according to package directions may be used, but they are usually very salty.

Chicken Broth

6 pounds chicken pieces
12 cups water
3 stalks celery with leaves, cut into 1-inch pieces
2 carrots, scraped and cut into 1-inch pieces
2 medium onions, quartered
1 bay leaf
¾ teaspoon salt
¾ teaspoon pepper
¾ teaspoon dried thyme

Combine all ingredients in a large Dutch oven. Bring to a boil; cover, reduce heat, and simmer 2 hours. Strain broth through a cheesecloth- or paper towel-lined sieve. Reserve chicken and vegetables for other uses; discard bay leaf. Cover and chill. Yield: 12 (1-cup) servings.

PER SERVING: 22 CALORIES (0% FROM FAT)
FAT 0.0G (SATURATED FAT 0.0G)
PROTEIN 0.5G CARBOHYDRATE 2.1G
CHOLESTEROL 0MG SODIUM 151MG

Fish Stock

3 pounds fish bones
4 cups water
2 cups dry white wine
3 (8-ounce) bottles clam juice
2 carrots, scraped and sliced
2 stalks celery with leaves, sliced
2 onions, sliced
8 black peppercorns
6 sprigs fresh parsley
4 whole cloves
1 lemon, halved
1 bay leaf

Combine all ingredients in a large Dutch oven. Bring to a boil; cover, reduce heat, and simmer 30 minutes. Strain stock through a cheesecloth- or paper towel-lined sieve. Cover and chill thoroughly. Yield: 8 (1-cup) servings.

PER SERVING: 10 CALORIES (18% FROM FAT)
FAT 0.2G (SATURATED FAT 0.0G)
PROTEIN 1.0G CARBOHYDRATE 1.3G
CHOLESTEROL 0MG SODIUM 250MG

Brown Veal Stock

5 pounds veal bones
6 quarts water
1¼ pounds carrots, sliced
3 medium onions, peeled and quartered
5 stalks celery, cut into pieces
4 cloves garlic, halved
5 bay leaves, crumbled
1 large bunch fresh parsley

Place veal bones in a shallow roasting pan. Bake at 450° for 45 minutes or until bones are well browned, turning occasionally. Combine browned bones and water in a 14-quart Dutch oven or stockpot. Cover; cook over medium-low 1½ hours. Uncover and simmer 4 hours, skimming surface frequently with a metal spoon to remove foam.

Add carrot, onion, celery, garlic, and bay leaves; arrange parsley on top. Reduce heat to low. Cook, uncovered, 6 hours. Remove from heat, and cool. Strain stock through a cheesecloth- or paper towel-lined sieve into a large bowl; discard bones and vegetables. Cover and chill stock. Skim solidified fat from top of stock, and discard. Yield: 4 (1-cup) servings.

Note: Avoid overbrowning veal bones; this will damage the stock's flavor.

PER SERVING: 22 CALORIES (0% FROM FAT)
FAT 0.0G (SATURATED FAT 0.0G)
PROTEIN 0.5G CARBOHYDRATE 1.9G
CHOLESTEROL 0MG SODIUM 7MG

Brown veal bones for a dark-colored stock.

WHAT ABOUT LEFTOVERS?

Fresh broth or stock can be refrigerated only three to four days, but that's no reason not to make large quantities of it. Freeze the broth in containers of various sizes—anything from 1 cup to 1 quart. You'll also find it handy to freeze broth in ice cube trays; transfer the cubes to a zip-top freezer bag once frozen. Each cube yields about 2 tablespoons of broth.

Freeze stock in ice cube trays.

Often recipes for soups and stews yield several servings—maybe more than you would want to use over a two- or three-day period. Most can be frozen successfully for later use. Thick gumbos, chilies, stews, and most soups that have a broth base tend to freeze especially well.

Freeze any remaining servings of soup in airtight plastic freezer containers or zip-top freezer bags, and label with the date the item was frozen. Use within three to four months for optimum flavor.

Thaw frozen soups at room temperature until still icy. Refrigerate until ready to serve, and then bring just to a simmer.

Following are some types of soups and stews that do not freeze well.

• Don't freeze any soup containing gumbo filé; the powder can turn stringy when it thaws.

• Avoid freezing soups that contain milk or cheese; dairy products often curdle when frozen and thawed, causing an unattractive appearance in the soup.

• Try not to freeze soups containing potatoes, since they tend to fall apart when thawed.

SOUP POTPOURRI

• **Menu Planning**—The yields for the soups and stews in this book are considered average-size servings. For an appetizer or dessert course, ¾ to 1 cup of soup is usually allowed. Yields for main-dish recipes may be from 1 to 2 cups per serving. The larger yields are recommended for soups that are served as one-dish meals with only bread or salad on the side.

• **Creative Concoctions**—Unlike some dishes, most soup recipes don't have to be followed precisely. You can usually add a little more or a little less of what's called for in the recipe, or you can make substitutions or additions of similar ingredients. You can even use meat, vegetable, rice, or pasta leftovers when making soups and stews.

• **Bouquet Garni**—When soups call for a large number of whole herbs and spices, it is helpful to confine the spices in a small bag made from cheesecloth. Called a bouquet garni, the filled spice bag allows you to easily remove the spices after the soup is cooked.

• **Spirited Soups**—Cook with wines and other spirits to add flavor but no fat. Most of the alcohol and calories will evaporate during cooking, leaving only the flavor behind.

• **Finishing Touches**—Keep garnishes simple. A sprinkling of chopped fresh herbs or green onions adds color to any soup, and croutons offer a little crunch. A slice of lemon, grated Parmesan cheese, or finely chopped cooked egg white can add interest to many soups.

• **Microwave Magic**—Many soups with complicated procedures and large yields can actually take longer to cook in the microwave than on the stovetop. But the microwave can certainly be useful for reheating small quantities of leftovers. Cooking times will vary according to the ingredients in the soup and the amount of soup to be reheated.

• **Unique Soup Bowls**—Don't fall into the routine of always serving your homemade soups from bowls in the kitchen. Offer steaming mugs of soup in the living room or in front of the den fireplace. Sip cold soups from chilled wine glasses or punch cups.

LOW-FAT BASICS

*W*hether you are trying to lose or maintain weight, low-fat eating makes good sense. Research studies show that decreasing your fat intake reduces risks of heart disease, diabetes, and some types of cancer. The goal recommended by major health groups is a fat intake of 30 percent or less of total daily calories.

The *Low-Fat Ways To Cook* series helps you meet that goal. Each book gives you practical, delicious recipes with realistic advice about low-fat cooking and eating. The recipes are lower in total fat than traditional recipes, and most provide less than 30 percent from fat and less than 10 percent from saturated fat.

If you have one high-fat item during a meal, you can balance it with low-fat choices for the rest of the day and still remain within the recommended percentage. For example, fat contributes 35 percent of the calories in the Chocolate Pound Cake for the Music and Dinner Alfresco menu beginning on page 23. However, the total menu provides only 15 percent of calories as fat.

The goal of fat reduction is not to eliminate fat entirely. In fact, a small amount of fat is needed to transport fat-soluble vitamins and maintain other normal body functions.

FIGURING THE FAT

The easiest way to achieve a diet with 30 percent or fewer of total calories from fat is to establish a daily "fat budget" based on the total number of calories you need each day. To estimate your daily calorie requirements, multiply your current weight by 15. Remember that this is only a rough guide because calorie requirements vary according to age, body size, and level of activity. To gain or lose 1 pound a week, add or subtract 500 calories a day. (A diet of fewer than 1,200 calories a day is not recommended unless medically supervised.)

Once you determine your calorie requirement, it's easy to figure the number of fat grams you should consume each day. These should equal or be lower than the number of fat grams indicated on the Daily Fat Limits chart.

DAILY FAT LIMITS		
Calories Per Day	30 Percent of Calories	Grams of Fat
1,200	360	40
1,500	450	50
1,800	540	60
2,000	600	67
2,200	660	73
2,500	750	83
2,800	840	93

NUTRITIONAL ANALYSIS

Each recipe in *Low-Fat Ways To Cook Soups and Stews* has been kitchen-tested by a staff of qualified home economists. In addition, registered dietitians have determined the nutrient information, using a computer system that analyzes every ingredient. These efforts ensure the success of each recipe and will help you fit these recipes into your own meal planning.

The nutrient grid that follows each recipe provides calories per serving and the percentage of calories from fat. In addition, the grid lists the grams of total fat, saturated fat, protein, and carbohydrate, and the milligrams of cholesterol and sodium per serving. The nutrient values are as accurate as possible and are based on these assumptions.

• When the recipe calls for cooked pasta, rice, or noodles, we base the analysis on cooking without additional salt or fat.

• The calculations indicate that meat and poultry are trimmed of fat and skin before cooking.

• Only the amount of marinade absorbed by the food is calculated.

• Garnishes and other optional ingredients are not calculated.

• Some of the alcohol calories evaporate during heating, and only those remaining are calculated.

• When a range is given for an ingredient (3 to 3½ cups, for instance), we calculate the lesser amount.

• Fruits and vegetables listed in the ingredients are not peeled unless specified.

Turkey-Black Bean Chili, Wilted Bacon Salad, and Buttermilk Corn Muffins (menu on page 18)

SENSIBLE DINNERS

Some of the most versatile menu items are soups and stews. A light soup served as a first course is a great way to take the edge off your appetite. And many other soups, stews, and chowders are filling enough to be considered one-dish meals.

In fact, soups and stews fit into almost any type of meal plan, as this chapter demonstrates. Start with Savory Carrot Soup (served hot or cold) as the appetizer for the festive menu on page 23. For a soup-and-sandwich combo, turn to page 14 where Baked Potato Soup is paired with pita sandwiches. When you prepare hearty Chick-Pea Tomato Soup (page 17) or Turkey-Black Bean Chili (page 18), all you'll need is a salad and bread to round out the meal.

LATE-NIGHT SUPPER

It's been a long day, and you're both tired. What could be more comforting than a hearty soup and sandwich? Afterward, serve a simple strawberry dessert.

Baked Potato Soup

Roasted Vegetable Pitas with Sour Cream Dressing

Marinated Strawberries in Orange Liqueur

Serves 2
TOTAL CALORIES PER SERVING: 551
(CALORIES FROM FAT: 21%)

BAKED POTATO SOUP

½ pound baking potatoes, peeled and cubed
1 cup 2% low-fat milk
1 teaspoon reduced-calorie margarine
⅛ teaspoon salt
⅛ teaspoon pepper
2 tablespoons sliced green onions
Bottled real bacon bits (optional)

Place potato in a saucepan; cover with water, and bring to a boil. Cook 15 minutes or until very tender; drain. Return potato to pan; mash to desired consistency. Add next 4 ingredients. Cook over medium heat until heated, stirring frequently.

Top each serving evenly with green onions and bacon bits, if desired. Yield: *2 (1-cup) servings.*

PER SERVING: 163 CALORIES (20% FROM FAT)
FAT 3.7G (SATURATED FAT 1.5G)
PROTEIN 6.5G CARBOHYDRATE 26.8G
CHOLESTEROL 10MG SODIUM 228MG

Baked Potato Soup and Roasted Vegetable Pitas with Sour Cream Dressing

Roasted Vegetable Pitas with Sour Cream Dressing

You can also use eggplant, yellow squash, and sweet red pepper in this sandwich. Feel free to experiment.

2 tablespoons (½ ounce) crumbled feta cheese
2 tablespoons nonfat sour cream
2 tablespoons skim milk
½ teaspoon prepared horseradish
Dash of pepper
1 cup sliced zucchini
1 cup (1-inch) pieces green pepper
½ teaspoon dried oregano
⅛ teaspoon salt
1½ teaspoons olive oil
1 large tomato (about 8 ounces), cut into 8 wedges
1 medium onion (about 8 ounces), cut into 8 wedges
2 cloves garlic, minced
Vegetable cooking spray
2 (6-inch) pita bread rounds, each cut in half

Combine first 5 ingredients in a small bowl; stir well, and set dressing aside.

Combine zucchini and next 7 ingredients in a medium bowl; toss gently. Spoon vegetable mixture onto a broiler pan coated with cooking spray. Broil 5½ inches from heat (with electric oven door partially opened) 10 minutes or until tender and lightly browned, stirring occasionally.

Divide vegetable mixture evenly between pita halves. Drizzle sour cream dressing evenly over each sandwich. Yield: 2 servings.

Per Serving: 296 Calories (22% from Fat)
Fat 7.2g (Saturated Fat 1.7g)
Protein 9.0g   Carbohydrate 49.1g
Cholesterol 7mg   Sodium 515mg

Marinated Strawberries in Orange Liqueur

This recipe combines the sweet flavor of the strawberry and the tangy taste of orange.

1 cup quartered strawberries
1 teaspoon sugar
2 teaspoons Grand Marnier or other orange-flavored liqueur, divided
¼ cup vanilla low-fat frozen yogurt, softened
⅓ cup frozen reduced-calorie whipped topping, thawed
½ teaspoon lemon juice

Combine strawberries, sugar, and 1 teaspoon liqueur in a bowl; toss gently. Cover and chill.

Place frozen yogurt in a bowl, and stir until smooth; fold in whipped topping. Add remaining liqueur and lemon juice; stir well.

Spoon ½ cup strawberry mixture into 2 individual dessert dishes, and top with ¼ cup yogurt mixture. Yield: 2 servings.

Per Serving: 92 Calories (21% from Fat)
Fat 2.1g (Saturated Fat 1.3g)
Protein 1.4g   Carbohydrate 15.3g
Cholesterol 2mg   Sodium 16mg

Did You Know?

The recommendation to eat five servings of fruits and vegetables a day isn't the old "eat lemons so you don't get scurvy" advice. Researchers now know that these foods contain vitamin C, beta carotene, and phytochemicals, which can help prevent a variety of diseases. One serving consists of a medium piece of fruit or ½ cup of cubed fruit. And fruit's benefits are greater when you eat whole fruit versus drinking a glass of juice.

SAVORY SOUP—VEGETARIAN STYLE

For a quick vegetarian meal, put on a pot of soup and toss a salad. The soup can simmer while you combine the greens and sauté the mushrooms for the Mushroom Crostini salad. Cooking the mushrooms with garlic and olive oil brings out their rich, earthy, almost meatlike flavor. Round out the menu with a medley of poached dried fruits that you can prepare a day or more ahead.

Chick-Pea Tomato Soup

Mushroom Crostini

Poached Dried Fruit

Serves 6

TOTAL CALORIES PER SERVING: 579
(CALORIES FROM FAT: 14%)

Chick-Pea Tomato Soup

CHICK-PEA TOMATO SOUP

Vegetable cooking spray
2 teaspoons olive oil
¾ cup chopped onion
¾ cup sliced celery
1 clove garlic, crushed
1 cup water
3 (14½-ounce) cans no-salt-added whole
    tomatoes, undrained and chopped
1 (14½-ounce) can vegetable broth
1 bay leaf
3 cups torn fresh spinach
2½ cups canned chick-peas (garbanzo beans)
¼ cup finely chopped fresh parsley
½ teaspoon freshly ground pepper
¼ cup grated Parmesan cheese
Fresh parsley sprigs (optional)

Coat a Dutch oven with cooking spray; add oil.
Place over medium-high heat until hot. Add onion,
celery, and garlic; sauté 8 minutes. Add water and
next 3 ingredients. Bring to a boil; cover, reduce
heat, and simmer 20 minutes. Add spinach and next
3 ingredients. Cook until heated. Ladle soup into
individual bowls; sprinkle with cheese. Garnish
with parsley, if desired. Yield: 6 (1¾-cup) servings.

PER SERVING: 208 CALORIES (21% FROM FAT)
FAT 4.8G (SATURATED FAT 1.1G)
PROTEIN 10.5G CARBOHYDRATE 33.3G
CHOLESTEROL 3MG SODIUM 496MG

MUSHROOM CROSTINI

Vegetable cooking spray
2 teaspoons olive oil, divided
2 (8-ounce) packages sliced fresh mushrooms
1 tablespoon minced fresh parsley
1½ teaspoons chopped fresh thyme
¼ teaspoon salt
¼ teaspoon freshly ground pepper
1 clove garlic, crushed
1 clove garlic, halved
6 cups mixed baby salad greens
1½ tablespoons lemon juice
6 (½-inch-thick) slices farmers' bread, toasted

Coat a large nonstick skillet with cooking spray;
add 1 teaspoon oil. Place over medium-high heat
until hot. Add sliced mushrooms, and sauté 3 minutes. Add parsley and next 4 ingredients; sauté 5
minutes. Set aside, and keep warm.

Rub the inside of a large bowl with cut sides of
halved garlic. Add remaining 1 teaspoon oil, greens,
and lemon juice to bowl; toss well. Arrange greens
on individual salad plates. Top bread slices with
mushroom mixture; place over greens. Yield: 6
servings.

Note: Substitute French or sourdough bread for
the farmers' bread, if desired.

PER SERVING: 135 CALORIES (19% FROM FAT)
FAT 2.8G (SATURATED FAT 0.3G)
PROTEIN 5.5G CARBOHYDRATE 23.4G
CHOLESTEROL 0MG SODIUM 316MG

POACHED DRIED FRUIT

2¾ cups unsweetened apple juice
1½ tablespoons lemon juice
6 whole cloves
2 (3-inch) sticks cinnamon
¾ cup pitted prunes
¾ cup dried apricots
1½ cups peeled, diced apple
1½ tablespoons orange zest
1 cup vanilla low-fat yogurt
1 tablespoon reduced-calorie maple syrup

Combine first 4 ingredients in a medium saucepan; bring to a boil. Add prunes and apricots; cover,
reduce heat, and simmer 15 minutes or until fruit is
tender. Add apple and orange zest; simmer 5 minutes. Remove and discard cloves and cinnamon
sticks. Let cool. Cover and chill.

Combine yogurt and syrup, stirring well. Spoon
fruit mixture into individual serving bowls. Top
with yogurt mixture. Yield: 6 servings.

PER SERVING: 236 CALORIES (6% FROM FAT)
FAT 1.6G (SATURATED FAT 0.4G)
PROTEIN 3.5G CARBOHYDRATE 57.1G
CHOLESTEROL 2MG SODIUM 45MG

TUNE IN FOR DINNER
(pictured on page 12)

On a cold winter night, home is the best place to be. So pair this speedy, casual supper with a favorite video for a cozy evening of entertainment. One whiff of this meal will tell family or friends that they're in for a treat.

The entire supper takes less than an hour to assemble. All the ingredients for the chili are full-flavored, so there's no need for a lengthy simmering time. Serve cornbread muffins (one per serving) with the chili.

Toss the salad just before serving, making sure the dressing is still warm. And remember to put the movie on pause long enough to serve dessert.

Turkey-Black Bean Chili

Wilted Bacon Salad

Buttermilk Corn Muffins

Cranberry-Apple Cobbler

Serves 5
TOTAL CALORIES PER SERVING: 598
(CALORIES FROM FAT: 11%)

TURKEY-BLACK BEAN CHILI

Vegetable cooking spray
1 cup coarsely chopped onion
½ cup sliced celery
2 (16-ounce) cans no-salt-added black beans, undrained
1 (10-ounce) can whole tomatoes and green chiles, undrained and chopped
6 ounces diced, cooked turkey breast
1 tablespoon chili seasoning mix
¼ cup plus 1 tablespoon nonfat sour cream
Sweet red pepper strips (optional)

Coat a small Dutch oven with cooking spray. Place over medium-high heat until hot. Add onion and celery; sauté until tender. Let cool slightly. Transfer mixture to container of an electric blender or food processor.

Drain beans, reserving liquid. Add half of beans and all of liquid to blender container. Cover and process until smooth, stopping once to scrape down sides. Return to Dutch oven.

Add remaining beans, tomatoes and chiles, turkey, and chili seasoning to Dutch oven. Cook over medium heat until heated. To serve, ladle chili into individual bowls; top each with 1 tablespoon sour cream. Garnish with pepper strips, if desired. Yield: 5 (1-cup) servings.

PER SERVING: 259 CALORIES (7% FROM FAT)
FAT 2.0G (SATURATED FAT 0.4G)
PROTEIN 22.7G   CARBOHYDRATE 36.1G
CHOLESTEROL 23MG   SODIUM 442MG

WILTED BACON SALAD

Using turkey bacon instead of regular bacon cuts the fat in this recipe by 2.2 grams per serving.

⅓ cup chopped onion
3 tablespoons brown sugar
3 tablespoons cider vinegar
4 slices turkey bacon, cooked and crumbled
7 cups mixed baby salad greens

Combine first 4 ingredients in a small saucepan; bring to a boil. Reduce heat; simmer, uncovered, 5 minutes, stirring until sugar dissolves.

Place salad greens in a large bowl; pour vinegar mixture over greens, tossing gently. Serve warm. Yield: 5 (1¼-cup) servings.

PER SERVING: 50 CALORIES (14% FROM FAT)
FAT 0.8G (SATURATED FAT 0.2G)
PROTEIN 1.3G CARBOHYDRATE 9.8G
CHOLESTEROL 3MG SODIUM 75MG

BUTTERMILK CORN MUFFINS

¾ cup yellow cornmeal
¾ cup all-purpose flour
1½ teaspoons baking powder
¼ teaspoon baking soda
¼ teaspoon salt
2 teaspoons sugar
1 cup nonfat buttermilk
¼ cup frozen egg substitute, thawed
1 tablespoon vegetable oil
½ cup canned no-salt-added whole-kernel corn, drained
Vegetable cooking spray

Combine first 6 ingredients in a medium bowl, stirring well. Make a well in center of mixture. Combine buttermilk, egg substitute, and oil. Add to dry ingredients, stirring just until dry ingredients are moistened. Fold in corn.

Spoon batter into muffin pans coated with cooking spray, filling two-thirds full. Bake at 425° for 18 to 20 minutes or until muffins are golden. Remove muffins from pans immediately. Yield: 10 muffins.

PER MUFFIN: 106 CALORIES (15% FROM FAT)
FAT 1.8G (SATURATED FAT 0.4G)
PROTEIN 3.5G CARBOHYDRATE 18.7G
CHOLESTEROL 1MG SODIUM 127MG

CRANBERRY-APPLE COBBLER

Commercial whole-berry cranberry sauce adds a tangy twist to this cobbler without adding fat.

3 cups peeled, coarsely chopped Rome apple (about 2 medium)
Butter-flavored vegetable cooking spray
1 (16-ounce) can jellied whole-berry cranberry sauce
¼ cup unsweetened orange juice
⅓ cup quick-cooking oats, uncooked
¼ cup all-purpose flour
2½ tablespoons brown sugar
2 tablespoons reduced-calorie margarine, softened

Place chopped apple in an 8-inch square pan coated with cooking spray. Combine cranberry sauce and orange juice, stirring well. Spoon cranberry sauce mixture evenly over apple.

Combine oats, flour, and brown sugar; cut in margarine with a pastry blender until mixture resembles coarse meal. Sprinkle oat mixture evenly over cranberry mixture. Coat oat mixture with cooking spray. Bake at 375° for 35 minutes or until apple is tender. Let stand 10 minutes before serving. Yield: 8 servings.

PER SERVING: 183 CALORIES (13% FROM FAT)
FAT 2.6G (SATURATED FAT 0.4G)
PROTEIN 1.8G CARBOHYDRATE 40.0G
CHOLESTEROL 0MG SODIUM 46MG

Shellfish-Tomato Soup and Spicy Cheese-Filled Bread

CREOLE SPECIAL

This spicy Creole-style soup is a meal in a bowl and every seafood lover's delight. A cheese and chile pepper filling adds a colorful swirl to the bread. Menu analysis reflects 12 ounces beer and two slices bread per person.

Shellfish-Tomato Soup
Spicy Cheese-Filled Bread
Marbled Brownies
Light beer

Serves 12
TOTAL CALORIES PER SERVING: 699
(CALORIES FROM FAT: 20%)

SHELLFISH-TOMATO SOUP

36 small clams in shells, scrubbed
2 tablespoons cornmeal
Vegetable cooking spray
1 tablespoon vegetable oil
3 cups chopped green pepper
2 cups chopped onion
2 cups chopped celery
3 cloves garlic, minced
1 tablespoon sweet Hungarian paprika
1½ teaspoons dried oregano
1½ teaspoons dried thyme
½ teaspoon black pepper
¼ teaspoon ground red pepper
1 tablespoon sugar
6 (10½-ounce) cans low-sodium chicken broth
2 (16-ounce) cans crushed tomatoes
1 (6-ounce) can no-salt-added tomato paste
1½ pounds unpeeled medium-size fresh shrimp
3 tablespoons gumbo filé
2 tablespoons lime juice
3 cups cooked rice (cooked without salt or fat)
½ pound fresh lump crabmeat, drained
½ cup chopped fresh parsley
12 lime wedges

Place clams in a large bowl, and cover with cold water. Sprinkle with cornmeal, and let stand 30 minutes. Drain and rinse; set clams aside. Discard cornmeal.

Coat an 8-quart Dutch oven with cooking spray; add oil, and place over medium heat until hot. Add green pepper and next 3 ingredients; sauté 10 minutes. Add paprika and next 4 ingredients; cook over low heat 5 minutes, stirring occasionally.

Add sugar and next 3 ingredients; stir well. Bring to a boil; reduce heat, and simmer, uncovered, 20 minutes. While soup simmers, peel and devein shrimp. Add clams to soup; cook over medium-high heat 10 minutes or until clams open. (Discard any unopened clams.)

Stir shrimp, gumbo filé, and lime juice into soup; cook 2 minutes or until shrimp turn pink. Using a slotted spoon, remove clams from soup; set aside. Spoon ¼ cup rice into each individual serving bowl; ladle 1½ cups soup over rice in each bowl, and top each with 3 clams, about 2 tablespoons crabmeat, and 2 teaspoons parsley. Serve with lime wedges. Yield: 12 servings.

PER SERVING: 308 CALORIES (15% FROM FAT)
FAT 5.3G (SATURATED FAT 0.9G)
PROTEIN 31.8G CARBOHYDRATE 34.2G
CHOLESTEROL 134MG SODIUM 560MG

SPICY CHEESE-FILLED BREAD

2¾ cups bread flour, divided
1 teaspoon salt
1 package active dry yeast
1 teaspoon sugar
1 cup very warm water (120° to 130°)
1 tablespoon extra-virgin olive oil
Vegetable cooking spray
¼ cup minced fresh parsley
¼ cup (1 ounce) shredded sharp Cheddar
   cheese
¼ cup freshly grated Parmesan cheese
3 tablespoons minced jalapeño pepper
3 tablespoons minced green onions
1 tablespoon extra-virgin olive oil
⅛ teaspoon pepper
4 cloves garlic, minced
2 teaspoons water
1 egg white

Combine 1 cup flour, salt, yeast, and sugar in a large bowl; stir well. Add 1 cup very warm water and 1 tablespoon oil; stir until well blended. Add 1½ cups flour; stir until a soft dough forms.

Turn dough out onto a lightly floured surface, and knead until smooth and elastic (about 8 minutes). Add enough of remaining ¼ cup flour, 1 tablespoon at a time, to prevent dough from sticking to hands. Place dough in a large bowl coated with cooking spray, turning to coat top. Cover and let rise in a warm place (85°), free from drafts, 45 minutes or until doubled in bulk.

Punch dough down, and roll into a 15- x 10-inch rectangle on a lightly floured surface. Combine parsley and next 7 ingredients; stir well. Spread parsley mixture evenly over dough, leaving a ½-inch margin around edges. Roll up dough, starting at long side, pressing firmly to eliminate air pockets; pinch ends and seam to seal. Place roll, seam side down, on a large baking sheet coated with cooking spray. Using a sharp knife, make ¼-inch-deep diagonal slits 3 inches apart across top of loaf.

Cover and let rise in a warm place, free from drafts, about 35 minutes or until doubled in bulk. Combine 2 teaspoons water and egg white, and gently brush over dough. Bake at 375° for 30 minutes or until loaf is golden and sounds hollow when tapped. Cool on a wire rack. Yield: 32 (½-inch) slices.

PER SLICE: 61 CALORIES (24% FROM FAT)
FAT 1.6G (SATURATED FAT 0.5G)
PROTEIN 2.2G CARBOHYDRATE 9.3G
CHOLESTEROL 2MG SODIUM 96MG

MARBLED BROWNIES

1 cup sugar
⅔ cup unsweetened cocoa
⅓ cup all-purpose flour
½ teaspoon baking powder
¼ cup vegetable oil
1 teaspoon vanilla extract
¼ teaspoon peppermint extract
4 egg whites, lightly beaten
Vegetable cooking spray
6 ounces nonfat cream cheese
3 tablespoons sugar
1 tablespoon all-purpose flour
½ teaspoon vanilla extract
¼ teaspoon peppermint extract
1 egg white

Combine first 4 ingredients in a large mixing bowl; stir well. Combine oil and next 3 ingredients in a small bowl; add to dry ingredients, stirring well. Spread batter in an 8-inch square pan coated with cooking spray.

Combine cream cheese and remaining 5 ingredients in a medium bowl. Beat at low speed of an electric mixer until smooth. Spoon cream cheese mixture by tablespoonfuls over cocoa mixture. Cut through cream cheese and cocoa mixtures with a knife to create a marbled effect. Bake at 350° for 22 minutes or until a wooden pick inserted in center comes out almost clean. Let cool in pan on a wire rack. Cut into bars. Yield: 12 brownies.

PER BROWNIE: 174 CALORIES (27% FROM FAT)
FAT 5.2G (SATURATED FAT 1.2G)
PROTEIN 5.2G CARBOHYDRATE 26.0G
CHOLESTEROL 3MG SODIUM 109MG

MUSIC AND DINNER ALFRESCO

An outdoor concert sets the mood for dining under the stars. Begin with Savory Carrot Soup and French bread. You'll receive rave reviews with this main-dish salad, Grilled and Chilled Chicken-Rice Salad. For the encore, offer Chocolate Pound Cake. Menu calories include one slice of bread and one slice of cake per person.

Concert Coolers

Savory Carrot Soup

Grilled and Chilled Chicken-Rice Salad

Commercial French bread

Chocolate Pound Cake

Serves 6
TOTAL CALORIES PER SERVING: 687
(CALORIES FROM FAT: 15%)

Savory Carrot Soup

CONCERT COOLERS

2 cups dry white wine, chilled
1 cup unsweetened orange juice
1 cup cranberry juice cocktail
2 tablespoons sugar
2 cups club soda, chilled
Fresh mint sprigs (optional)

Combine wine, orange juice, cranberry juice cocktail, and sugar in a pitcher; stir well. Cover and chill. Just before serving, stir in club soda. Serve over ice. Garnish with mint sprigs, if desired. Yield: 6 (1-cup) servings.

PER SERVING: 110 CALORIES (0% FROM FAT)
FAT 0.0G (SATURATED FAT 0.0G)
PROTEIN 0.4G   CARBOHYDRATE 15.5G
CHOLESTEROL 0MG   SODIUM 21MG

SAVORY CARROT SOUP

Vegetable cooking spray
2 teaspoons reduced-calorie margarine
1½ cups chopped onion
2¾ cups sliced carrot
1½ cups diced red potato
3 cups canned no-salt-added chicken broth,
    undiluted
¾ cup unsweetened orange juice
½ teaspoon dried thyme
¼ teaspoon salt
¼ teaspoon pepper
Fresh thyme sprigs (optional)

Coat a large saucepan with cooking spray; add margarine, and place over medium-high heat until margarine melts. Add onion and carrot; sauté until crisp-tender. Add potato and chicken broth; bring to a boil. Cover, reduce heat, and simmer 25 minutes or until carrot is tender. Let cool slightly.

Transfer carrot mixture in batches to container of an electric blender or food processor; cover and process 1 minute or until mixture is smooth, stopping once to scrape down sides.

Return carrot mixture to saucepan; add orange juice, dried thyme, salt, and pepper. Cook, uncovered, until thoroughly heated. Serve warm or chilled. Garnish with fresh thyme, if desired. Yield: 6 (1-cup) servings.

PER SERVING: 112 CALORIES (17% FROM FAT)
FAT 2.1G (SATURATED FAT 0.5G)
PROTEIN 3.2G   CARBOHYDRATE 20.6G
CHOLESTEROL 0MG   SODIUM 206MG

GRILLED AND CHILLED CHICKEN-RICE SALAD

4 (4-ounce) skinned, boned chicken breast
    halves
1 tablespoon low-sodium soy sauce
½ teaspoon salt-free lemon-pepper seasoning
Vegetable cooking spray
1 cup chopped Red Delicious apple
2 teaspoons lemon juice
2½ cups cooked long-grain rice (cooked
    without salt or fat)
¾ cup sliced celery
⅓ cup raisins
¼ cup plus 2 tablespoons nonfat mayonnaise
¼ cup plain nonfat yogurt
¼ cup unsweetened apple juice
Lettuce leaves (optional)
¼ cup thinly sliced green onions

Brush chicken with soy sauce, and sprinkle with lemon-pepper seasoning.

Coat grill rack with cooking spray, and place on grill over medium-hot coals (350° to 400°). Place chicken on rack, and grill 5 to 6 minutes on each side or until chicken is done. Remove chicken from grill, and let cool slightly. Cut chicken into 1-inch pieces.

Combine chopped apple and lemon juice in a large bowl. Add chicken, cooked rice, celery, and raisins to apple mixture; toss well.

Combine mayonnaise, yogurt, and apple juice in a small bowl; stir well. Pour mayonnaise mixture over chicken mixture, and toss gently to combine. Cover and chill thoroughly.

Just before serving, spoon mixture into a lettuce-lined bowl, if desired. Sprinkle with green onions. Yield: 6 (1-cup) servings.

PER SERVING: 232 CALORIES (10% FROM FAT)
FAT 2.5G (SATURATED FAT 0.7G)
PROTEIN 19.8G   CARBOHYDRATE 33.3G
CHOLESTEROL 47MG   SODIUM 318MG

rack. Sift powdered sugar over cooled cake. Cut into ½-inch slices. Garnish with fresh strawberries, if desired. Yield: 16 servings.

PER SERVING: 160 CALORIES (35% FROM FAT)
FAT 6.2G (SATURATED FAT 1.2G)
PROTEIN 2.9G   CARBOHYDRATE 23.1G
CHOLESTEROL 1MG   SODIUM 162MG

CHOCOLATE POUND CAKE

Vegetable cooking spray
2¼ cups plus 1 teaspoon sifted cake flour, divided
½ cup margarine, softened
¾ cup sugar
3 egg whites
2 teaspoons vanilla extract
¼ cup unsweetened cocoa
¾ teaspoon baking soda
¼ teaspoon salt
1 (8-ounce) carton vanilla low-fat yogurt
1 teaspoon powdered sugar
Fresh strawberries (optional)

Coat bottom and sides of an 8½- x 4½- x 3-inch loafpan with cooking spray; sprinkle with 1 teaspoon flour, and set aside.

Beat margarine at medium speed of an electric mixer until creamy; gradually add sugar, beating well. Add egg whites; beat 4 minutes or until well blended. Stir in vanilla.

Combine remaining 2¼ cups flour, cocoa, soda, and salt; add to creamed mixture alternately with yogurt, beginning and ending with dry ingredients.

Pour batter into prepared pan. Bake at 350° for 55 to 60 minutes or until a wooden pick inserted in center comes out clean. Cool in pan 10 minutes; remove from pan. Let cool completely on a wire

Chocolate Pound Cake

Summer Gazpacho (recipe on page 30)

ON THE COOL SIDE

*W*hen summertime arrives and the temperatures soar, a bowl of chilled soup is a welcome appetizer or sandwich accompaniment. Made with naturally low-fat vegetables or fruit, cold soups are both refreshing and nutritious.

Soup for dessert? Why not, if it's made with melon, strawberries, peaches, or other sweet fruits. Chilled Apricot-Pear Soup (page 34) is the first of several such creations, any of which is appropriate for either starting or ending a meal.

As delicious as they are, chilled soups have traditionally been high in fat. However, the recipes in this chapter make use of low-fat or nonfat dairy products such as skim milk, yogurt, or sour cream to give the soup a creamy consistency without adding much fat.

Chilled Borscht

CHILLED BORSCHT

2 cups canned low-sodium chicken broth,
    undiluted
½ cup water
¾ cup minced carrot
¼ cup minced onion
¼ cup minced celery
¼ cup Zinfandel or other sweet red wine
1 (16-ounce) can whole beets, undrained
1 teaspoon lemon juice
⅛ teaspoon salt
⅛ teaspoon ground white pepper
Fresh chive sprigs (optional)

  Combine first 5 ingredients in a medium
saucepan. Bring mixture to a boil; cover, reduce
heat, and simmer 20 minutes or until vegetables
are tender. Add wine, and cook 1 minute. Remove
from heat, and let cool.

  Combine half of vegetable mixture, half of beets,
lemon juice, salt, and pepper in container of an
electric blender or food processor. Cover and
process until smooth. Transfer mixture to a medium
bowl; repeat procedure with remaining vegetable
mixture and beets. Combine pureed mixtures, and
stir well. Cover and chill thoroughly.

  To serve, ladle soup into individual bowls. Garnish with fresh chive sprigs, if desired. Yield: 8
(¾-cup) servings.

PER SERVING: 35 CALORIES (3% FROM FAT)
FAT 0.1G (SATURATED FAT 0.0G)
PROTEIN 0.9G CARBOHYDRATE 7.4G
CHOLESTEROL 0MG SODIUM 179MG

CURRIED BROCCOLI SOUP

Vegetable cooking spray
1 cup chopped onion
1 teaspoon curry powder
¼ teaspoon salt
6 cups chopped fresh broccoli
2½ cups canned no-salt-added chicken broth,
    undiluted
1 cup nonfat buttermilk
¼ cup plus 1 tablespoon low-fat sour cream

Coat a large saucepan with cooking spray; place over medium heat until hot. Add onion, and sauté until tender. Stir in curry powder and salt; cook 1 minute. Add broccoli and chicken broth; stir well. Bring to a boil; reduce heat, and simmer, uncovered, 20 minutes or until broccoli is very tender. Let mixture cool slightly.

Transfer broccoli mixture in batches to container of an electric blender or food processor; cover and process until smooth. Pour pureed mixture into a large bowl; add buttermilk to broccoli mixture, and stir well. Cover and chill.

Ladle soup into individual bowls; top each with 1 tablespoon sour cream. Yield: 5 (1-cup) servings.

PER SERVING: 95 CALORIES (25% FROM FAT)
FAT 2.6G (SATURATED FAT 1.4G)
PROTEIN 6.1G CARBOHYDRATE 12.8G
CHOLESTEROL 8MG SODIUM 209MG

Curried Broccoli Soup

CUCUMBER VICHYSSOISE

Vegetable cooking spray
1 teaspoon reduced-calorie margarine
3 cups sliced leeks
2 cups sliced onion
2⅓ cups peeled, seeded, and coarsely chopped
    cucumber
1 cup water
2 cups peeled, cubed baking potato
2 cups canned no-salt-added chicken broth,
    undiluted
½ teaspoon salt
½ teaspoon ground white pepper
1 cup 1% low-fat milk
Thinly sliced cucumber (optional)
Chopped fresh chives (optional)

Coat a large Dutch oven with cooking spray; add margarine. Place over medium-high heat until margarine melts. Add leeks and onion; sauté 15 minutes or until vegetables are tender and golden.

Combine chopped cucumber and water in a small saucepan; bring to a boil. Cover, reduce heat, and simmer 10 minutes.

Add cooked cucumber and cooking liquid, potato, and next 3 ingredients to onion mixture in Dutch oven. Bring to a boil; cover, reduce heat, and simmer 10 minutes or until potato is tender. Remove from heat; let cool 10 minutes.

Transfer cucumber mixture in batches to container of an electric blender or food processor; cover and process until smooth. Pour pureed cucumber mixture into a large bowl. Add milk, and stir well.

Cover and chill thoroughly. Ladle soup into individual bowls. If desired, garnish with cucumber slices and chives. Yield: 8 (1-cup) servings.

PER SERVING: 90 CALORIES (14% FROM FAT)
FAT 1.4G (SATURATED FAT 0.4G)
PROTEIN 3.3G CARBOHYDRATE 16.6G
CHOLESTEROL 1MG SODIUM 211MG

ROASTED SWEET RED PEPPER GAZPACHO

2 teaspoons olive oil
1½ cups chopped onion
2½ pounds sweet red peppers, roasted, peeled, and coarsely chopped
½ teaspoon grated orange rind
3 cups low-sodium chicken broth, undiluted
1 tablespoon minced jalapeño pepper
2 tablespoons fresh lime juice
¼ teaspoon salt
¼ teaspoon ground white pepper
2 cloves garlic, minced
1 clove garlic, halved
5 (½-inch-thick) diagonally cut slices French bread baguette
Vegetable cooking spray
Chopped fresh cilantro (optional)

Heat oil in a large saucepan over medium-low heat. Add onion; cover and cook 15 minutes or until tender. Add sweet red pepper and orange rind; cover and cook 5 additional minutes, stirring occasionally. Add chicken broth, and bring to a boil. Partially cover, reduce heat, and simmer 20 minutes. Let mixture cool slightly.

Transfer mixture in batches to container of an electric blender or food processor; cover and process until smooth. Pour into a bowl, and stir in jalapeño pepper and next 4 ingredients. Cover mixture, and chill.

Rub cut sides of garlic halves over one side of each bread slice; discard garlic. Coat same side of bread with cooking spray; place on a baking sheet. Bake at 350° for 10 minutes or until browned.

To serve, ladle soup into individual bowls; sprinkle with cilantro, if desired. Serve with toasted bread. Yield: 5 (1-cup) servings.

PER SERVING: 127 CALORIES (28% FROM FAT)
FAT 4.0G (SATURATED FAT 0.7G)
PROTEIN 4.3G CARBOHYDRATE 20.7G
CHOLESTEROL 0MG SODIUM 236MG

SUMMER GAZPACHO

(pictured on page 26)

You can serve gazpacho as a refreshing first course or with sandwiches and fresh fruit for a complete light meal.

1 (10½-ounce) can low-sodium tomato soup
1¾ cups no-salt-added tomato juice
⅔ cup peeled, seeded, and finely chopped cucumber
½ cup finely chopped green pepper
½ cup finely chopped tomato
⅓ cup finely chopped onion
2 tablespoons red wine vinegar
1 tablespoon commercial oil-free Italian dressing
1 tablespoon lemon juice
½ teaspoon pepper
¼ teaspoon salt
¼ teaspoon hot sauce
1 clove garlic, minced
Thinly sliced cucumber (optional)

Combine tomato soup and next 12 ingredients in a large bowl; stir well. Cover soup, and chill at least 8 hours.

To serve, ladle soup into individual bowls, and garnish with cucumber slices, if desired. Yield: 5 (1-cup) servings.

PER SERVING: 75 CALORIES (17% FROM FAT)
FAT 1.4G (SATURATED FAT 0.0G)
PROTEIN 2.1G CARBOHYDRATE 15.2G
CHOLESTEROL 0MG SODIUM 174MG

FYI

When using an electric blender or food processor to puree soup ingredients, you may need to process the mixture in batches to avoid overflow. Allow cooked mixtures to cool slightly before processing.

Garden Gazpacho for Two

GARDEN GAZPACHO FOR TWO

Gazpacho is a cool way to start a south-of-the-border meal.

1¼ cups seeded, chopped tomato
1 cup low-sodium vegetable juice cocktail
¼ cup chopped cucumber
¼ cup chopped celery
¼ cup chopped green pepper
¼ cup sliced green onions
1 tablespoon lemon juice
1 tablespoon commercial oil-free Italian
    dressing
⅛ teaspoon salt
⅛ teaspoon garlic powder
⅛ teaspoon pepper
⅛ teaspoon hot sauce
Fresh chive blossoms (optional)

Combine first 12 ingredients in a medium bowl. Cover and chill at least 6 hours.

To serve, ladle soup into individual bowls, and garnish with chive blossoms, if desired. Yield: 2 (1½-cup) servings.

PER SERVING: 75 CALORIES (8% FROM FAT)
FAT 0.7G (SATURATED FAT 0.1G)
PROTEIN 3.1G CARBOHYDRATE 16.3G
CHOLESTEROL 0MG SODIUM 285MG

CHILLED SPINACH AND CUCUMBER SOUP

2 teaspoons margarine
2 cups peeled, seeded, and cubed cucumber
2 cups canned low-sodium chicken broth, undiluted
2 cups tightly packed torn fresh spinach
1 teaspoon chopped fresh dill
⅛ teaspoon salt
⅛ teaspoon coarsely ground pepper
Dash of ground nutmeg
¾ cup nonfat sour cream, divided
½ cup plain nonfat yogurt
Thinly sliced unpeeled cucumber (optional)
Fresh dill sprigs (optional)

Melt margarine in a medium saucepan over medium heat. Add cucumber; sauté 10 minutes or until lightly browned. Add broth; bring to a boil. Cover, reduce heat, and simmer 15 minutes. Add spinach and next 4 ingredients; bring to a boil. Cover, reduce heat, and simmer 2 minutes. Let cool slightly.

Place cucumber mixture in container of an electric blender or food processor; cover and process until smooth. Pour into a bowl; add ½ cup sour cream and yogurt, stirring with a wire whisk. Cover and chill.

To serve, ladle soup into individual bowls; top each with 1 tablespoon sour cream. If desired, garnish with cucumber slices and dill sprigs. Yield: 4 (1-cup) servings.

PER SERVING: 95 CALORIES (27% FROM FAT)
FAT 2.9G (SATURATED FAT 0.7G)
PROTEIN 7.1G   CARBOHYDRATE 9.7G
CHOLESTEROL 1MG   SODIUM 212MG

Chilled Spinach and Cucumber Soup

COLD SQUASH SOUP

Vegetable cooking spray
1 tablespoon reduced-calorie margarine
½ cup minced onion
1 clove garlic, minced
7 cups thinly sliced yellow squash (about 8 small)
1 small potato (about 4 ounces), peeled and cubed
2 cups canned no-salt-added chicken broth, undiluted
¾ cup 1% low-fat milk
2 teaspoons minced fresh thyme
¼ teaspoon salt
⅛ teaspoon ground white pepper
Fresh thyme sprigs (optional)

Coat a large nonstick skillet with cooking spray; add margarine. Place over medium-high heat until margarine melts. Add minced onion and garlic; sauté until tender. Add squash slices, potato cubes, and chicken broth. Bring mixture to a boil; cover, reduce heat, and simmer 15 minutes or until vegetables are tender. Let cool slightly.

Transfer mixture in batches to container of an electric blender or food processor; cover and process until smooth. Pour mixture into a large bowl. Stir in milk, minced thyme, salt, and pepper. Cover and chill thoroughly.

To serve, ladle soup into individual bowls. Garnish with thyme sprigs, if desired. Yield: 6 (1-cup) servings.

PER SERVING: 78 CALORIES (23% FROM FAT)
FAT 2.0G (SATURATED FAT 0.4G)
PROTEIN 3.3G CARBOHYDRATE 12.5G
CHOLESTEROL 1MG SODIUM 137MG

CHILLED ZUCCHINI BISQUE

3 cups canned low-sodium chicken broth, undiluted
2 cups diced zucchini
1 cup diced onion
1 cup peeled, diced potato
2 cloves garlic, minced
1 cup plain nonfat yogurt
1 cup peeled, seeded, and diced tomato
½ cup sliced green onions
2 tablespoons minced fresh parsley
2 tablespoons white wine vinegar
¼ teaspoon salt
¼ teaspoon dry mustard
⅛ teaspoon ground white pepper
3 drops of hot sauce

Combine broth, zucchini, onion, potato, and garlic in a large saucepan. Bring to a boil over high heat; cover, reduce heat, and simmer 15 minutes or until potato is tender. Let mixture cool slightly.

Transfer mixture in batches to container of an electric blender or food processor; cover and process until smooth. Pour into a bowl; let cool. Stir in yogurt and remaining ingredients. Cover and chill. Yield: 6 (1-cup) servings.

PER SERVING: 72 CALORIES (5% FROM FAT)
FAT 0.4G (SATURATED FAT 0.1G)
PROTEIN 4.1G CARBOHYDRATE 12.6G
CHOLESTEROL 1MG SODIUM 140MG

FRESH TOMATO SOUP WITH CILANTRO

1 cup vertically sliced onion
Vegetable cooking spray
1 teaspoon olive oil
¼ cup thinly sliced celery
1 small clove garlic, minced
1 teaspoon ground cumin
½ teaspoon salt
⅛ to ¼ teaspoon pepper
4 cups peeled, coarsely chopped tomato (about 2¼ pounds)
⅓ cup water
1 (14¼-ounce) can no-salt-added chicken broth
2 tablespoons chopped fresh cilantro
Fresh cilantro sprigs (optional)

Cut onion slices in half. Coat a large saucepan with cooking spray; add oil, and place over medium heat until hot. Add onion, celery, and garlic; sauté 5 minutes or until tender. Add cumin, salt, and pepper; cook 5 minutes, stirring often. Add tomato, water, and chicken broth; bring to a boil. Reduce heat, and simmer, uncovered, 10 minutes. Let mixture cool slightly.

Place 2½ cups tomato mixture in container of an electric blender or food processor; cover and process until smooth. Add tomato puree back to mixture in pan, and stir well. Add chopped cilantro, and stir well.

Serve warm or chilled; garnish with fresh cilantro sprigs, if desired. Yield: 6 (1-cup) servings.

PER SERVING: 49 CALORIES (26% FROM FAT)
FAT 1.4G (SATURATED FAT 0.2G)
PROTEIN 1.5G CARBOHYDRATE 8.3G
CHOLESTEROL 0MG SODIUM 214MG

Chilled Apricot-Pear Soup

CHILLED APRICOT-PEAR SOUP

1 (16-ounce) can apricot halves in juice,
    undrained
1 (16-ounce) can pear halves in juice,
    undrained
1 (8-ounce) carton vanilla low-fat yogurt
½ cup skim milk
2 tablespoons Grand Marnier or other
    orange-flavored liqueur
½ teaspoon ground cinnamon
¼ teaspoon ground nutmeg
⅛ teaspoon ground cloves
Fresh apricot slices (optional)
Fresh mint sprigs (optional)

Drain canned fruit, reserving 1 cup juice. Combine canned fruit, yogurt, and next 5 ingredients in container of an electric blender or food processor; cover and process 1 minute or until smooth, stopping once to scrape down sides. Add reserved 1 cup juice, stirring until blended. Cover and chill.

To serve, ladle soup into individual bowls. If desired, garnish with fresh apricot slices and mint sprigs. Yield: 6 (¾-cup) servings.

PER SERVING: 115 CALORIES (5% FROM FAT)
FAT 0.6G (SATURATED FAT 0.4G)
PROTEIN 3.2G   CARBOHYDRATE 23.1G
CHOLESTEROL 2MG   SODIUM 40MG

CHILLED BLUEBERRY SOUP

3 cups water, divided
4 cups fresh blueberries
3 tablespoons lemon juice
3 tablespoons crème de cassis
2 tablespoons Triple Sec or other
    orange-flavored liqueur
2 tablespoons honey
2 (1-inch) sticks cinnamon
2 tablespoons cornstarch
1 tablespoon plus 2 teaspoons low-fat sour
    cream
Orange zest (optional)

Combine 2½ cups water, blueberries, and next 5 ingredients in a large saucepan. Bring to a boil; cover, reduce heat, and simmer 15 minutes.

Combine cornstarch and remaining ½ cup water, stirring until smooth. Add cornstarch mixture to blueberry mixture; bring to a boil, and cook, stirring constantly, 1 minute. Remove from heat; let cool 15 minutes. Remove and discard cinnamon sticks.

Transfer blueberry mixture in batches to container of an electric blender or food processor; cover and process until mixture is smooth. Cover and chill thoroughly.

To serve, ladle soup into individual bowls. Top each serving with 1 teaspoon sour cream, and garnish with orange zest, if desired. Yield: 5 (1-cup) servings.

PER SERVING: 148 CALORIES (3% FROM FAT)
FAT 0.5G (SATURATED FAT 0.1G)
PROTEIN 1.4G   CARBOHYDRATE 37.0G
CHOLESTEROL 0MG   SODIUM 14MG

CHERRIES AND CREAM SOUP

2½ cups cherry juice, divided
3 tablespoons cornstarch
½ cup muscatel or other sweet white wine
1 tablespoon fresh lemon juice
⅓ cup nonfat sour cream
1 (16-ounce) package frozen sweet cherries,
    thawed

Combine ¼ cup cherry juice and cornstarch in a small bowl; stir well. Combine 1¼ cups cherry juice, wine, and lemon juice in a nonaluminum saucepan; cook over medium heat until warm. Stir in cornstarch mixture, and cook, stirring constantly, until thickened and bubbly. Transfer juice mixture to a bowl.

Combine remaining 1 cup cherry juice and sour cream in container of an electric blender or food processor; cover and process until smooth. Add to juice mixture in bowl, and stir well. Skim foam from top of juice mixture.

Chop cherries, reserving juice. Stir cherries and reserved juice into thickened juice mixture; stir well. Cover and chill at least 4 hours. Stir before serving. Yield: 5 (1-cup) servings.

PER SERVING: 170 CALORIES (5% FROM FAT)
FAT 0.9G (SATURATED FAT 0.2G)
PROTEIN 2.2G   CARBOHYDRATE 39.0G
CHOLESTEROL 0MG   SODIUM 13MG

When pureeing an especially thick or chunky soup mixture, scrape down the sides of the electric blender or food processor container one or more times during processing. This enables you to puree all of the mixture to a smooth consistency.

MINTED CANTALOUPE DESSERT SOUP

6 cups cubed cantaloupe (about 2 large),
   divided
¾ cup unsweetened orange juice
3 tablespoons lime juice
¼ teaspoon peppermint extract
1 (8-ounce) carton vanilla low-fat yogurt
2 teaspoons powdered sugar
2 tablespoons nonfat sour cream
Fresh mint sprigs (optional)

Place 3 cups cantaloupe, orange juice, lime juice, and peppermint extract in container of an electric blender or food processor; cover and process until smooth, stopping once to scrape down sides. Transfer puree to a large bowl. Place remaining 3 cups cantaloupe in blender container; cover and process until smooth. Add to pureed mixture in bowl.

Add yogurt and powdered sugar to cantaloupe mixture; stir well. Cover and chill. To serve, ladle soup into individual bowls. Top each serving with 1 teaspoon sour cream; garnish with mint sprigs, if desired. Yield: 6 (1-cup) servings.

PER SERVING: 122 CALORIES (7% FROM FAT)
FAT 1.0G (SATURATED FAT 0.6G)
PROTEIN 4.1G CARBOHYDRATE 26.2G
CHOLESTEROL 2MG SODIUM 46MG

CHILLED HONEYDEW SOUP

7 cups honeydew melon chunks (about 1
   medium)
⅓ cup unsweetened orange juice
¼ cup Sauternes or other sweet white wine
2 tablespoons lime juice
2 teaspoons powdered sugar
½ cup fresh raspberries
Fresh mint sprigs (optional)

Place half of honeydew in container of an electric blender or food processor; cover and process until smooth. Transfer puree to a large bowl. Repeat procedure with remaining honeydew. Combine honeydew, orange juice, and next 3 ingredients; stir well. Cover and chill thoroughly.

To serve, ladle soup into individual bowls, and top each with raspberries. Garnish with fresh mint sprigs, if desired. Yield: 6 (1-cup) servings.

PER SERVING: 86 CALORIES (3% FROM FAT)
FAT 0.3G (SATURATED FAT 0.1G)
PROTEIN 1.1G CARBOHYDRATE 22.2G
CHOLESTEROL 0MG SODIUM 21MG

MELON SWIRL SOUP

2 cups cubed cantaloupe
1 tablespoon honey
2 cups cubed honeydew melon
1 tablespoon lime juice

Combine cantaloupe and honey in container of an electric blender or food processor; cover and process 1 minute or until smooth. Pour into a bowl; cover and chill.

Combine honeydew and lime juice in container of an electric blender or food processor; cover and process 1 minute or until smooth. Pour into a bowl; cover and chill.

To serve, pour about ¼ cup plus 2 tablespoons of each melon mixture, side by side, into each of 4 bowls. Draw a wooden pick or knife through melon mixtures to make a swirl design. Serve immediately. Yield: 4 (¾-cup) servings.

PER SERVING: 75 CALORIES (4% FROM FAT)
FAT 0.3G (SATURATED FAT 0.2G)
PROTEIN 1.1G CARBOHYDRATE 19.2G
CHOLESTEROL 0MG SODIUM 16MG

CHILLED MELON SOUP

3 cups cubed honeydew melon
3 cups cubed cantaloupe
¼ cup vodka, divided
¼ cup firmly packed brown sugar, divided
1 tablespoon plus 1 teaspoon fresh lime juice, divided
¾ cup sliced fresh strawberries

Place honeydew in container of an electric blender or food processor. Cover and process until smooth; pour into a large bowl. Place cantaloupe in container of electric blender or food processor. Cover and process until smooth; pour into a large bowl. To each bowl of pureed melon, add 2 tablespoons vodka, 2 tablespoons brown sugar, and 2 teaspoons lime juice; stir well. Cover and chill.

Place strawberries in container of an electric blender or food processor; cover and process until smooth. Pour into a bowl; cover and chill.

To serve, pour ½ cup cantaloupe mixture into each of 4 individual bowls; pour ½ cup honeydew mixture in center of cantaloupe mixture. Dollop each serving with 2 tablespoons pureed strawberries; swirl decoratively with a wooden pick. Yield: 4 (1-cup) servings.

PER SERVING: 181 CALORIES (3% FROM FAT)
FAT 0.6G (SATURATED FAT 0.3G)
PROTEIN 1.8G   CARBOHYDRATE 37.5G
CHOLESTEROL 0MG   SODIUM 29MG

Chilled Melon Soup

Tropical Soup

TROPICAL SOUP

4 cups peeled, chopped mango
¾ cup unsweetened apple juice
2 teaspoons honey
1 teaspoon vanilla extract
¼ teaspoon ground allspice
⅛ teaspoon ground cinnamon
¾ cup evaporated skimmed milk
¼ cup plus 2 tablespoons vanilla low-fat
    yogurt
Strawberry halves (optional)
Fresh mint sprigs (optional)

Combine first 6 ingredients in container of an electric blender or food processor; cover and process until smooth, stopping once to scrape down sides of container.

Transfer mango mixture to a large bowl. Stir in milk and yogurt. Cover and chill at least 30 minutes. Ladle soup into individual bowls. If desired, garnish with strawberry halves and mint sprigs. Yield: 5 (1-cup) servings.

PER SERVING: 184 CALORIES (4% FROM FAT)
FAT 0.8G (SATURATED FAT 0.3G)
PROTEIN 4.6G   CARBOHYDRATE 43.0G
CHOLESTEROL 2MG   SODIUM 60MG

FRESH MELON, PEACH, AND BLUEBERRY SOUP

3 cups diced honeydew melon
½ cup fresh orange juice
½ cup vanilla low-fat yogurt
1 tablespoon honey
1 teaspoon peeled, finely chopped gingerroot
2 teaspoons fresh lime juice
2 cups peeled, diced peaches (about 1½
    pounds)
1 cup fresh blueberries

Place first 6 ingredients in container of an electric blender or food processor; cover and process until smooth. Combine melon mixture, diced peaches, and blueberries in a bowl; stir well. Cover and chill thoroughly. Yield: 6 (1-cup) servings.

PER SERVING: 107 CALORIES (4% FROM FAT)
FAT 0.5G (SATURATED FAT 0.2G)
PROTEIN 2.1G   CARBOHYDRATE 26.0G
CHOLESTEROL 1MG   SODIUM 23MG

MED-RIM FRUIT SOUP

2 cups diced plums
2 cups peeled, diced peaches
2 cups diced cantaloupe
2 cups apricot nectar
¾ cup Moscato d'Asti or other sweet sparkling
    wine
¼ cup water
2 tablespoons honey
1 (3-inch) cinnamon stick
1 bay leaf
Pomegranate seeds (optional)

Combine first 3 ingredients in a large bowl; set aside. Combine nectar and next 5 ingredients in a medium saucepan; bring to a boil. Cover, reduce heat, and simmer 10 minutes. Discard cinnamon and bay leaf. Pour nectar mixture over fruit; cover and chill.

To serve, ladle soup into individual bowls; garnish with pomegranate seeds, if desired. Yield: 7 (1-cup) servings.

PER SERVING: 124 CALORIES (4% FROM FAT)
FAT 0.5G (SATURATED FAT 0.1G)
PROTEIN 1.5G   CARBOHYDRATE 31.2G
CHOLESTEROL 0MG   SODIUM 9MG

Minted Peach and Champagne Soup and Fresh Raspberry Soup

MINTED PEACH AND CHAMPAGNE SOUP

3 pounds fresh peaches, peeled, pitted, and
    coarsely chopped
½ cup peach nectar
¼ cup water
1 tablespoon sugar
1½ tablespoons lemon juice
¼ teaspoon ground cinnamon
⅛ teaspoon ground ginger
¼ cup loosely packed fresh mint leaves
1¼ cups champagne, chilled
Fresh peach slices (optional)
Fresh mint sprigs (optional)

Combine first 7 ingredients in a medium
saucepan. Bring to a boil; cover, reduce heat, and
simmer 10 to 15 minutes or until peaches are tender. Remove from heat; let mixture cool slightly.
Add ¼ cup mint leaves.

Transfer peach mixture in batches to container
of an electric blender or food processor. Cover and
process until smooth. Transfer to a large bowl.
Cover and chill thoroughly.

To serve, add champagne to peach mixture; stir
gently. Ladle soup into individual bowls. If
desired, garnish with peach slices and mint sprigs.
Yield: 6 (1-cup) servings.

PER SERVING: 136 CALORIES (1% FROM FAT)
FAT 0.2G (SATURATED FAT 0.0G)
PROTEIN 1.5G   CARBOHYDRATE 26.2G
CHOLESTEROL 0MG   SODIUM 4MG

BLUSHING PEAR SOUP

Serve this soup as a refreshing first course or as a light dessert.

½ cup sugar
1½ cups water
1½ cups port wine
2 teaspoons grated lemon rind
½ teaspoon lemon juice
3 whole cloves
1 (3-inch) stick cinnamon
6 ripe pears, peeled, cored, and sliced
½ cup low-fat sour cream
Ground cinnamon (optional)

Combine first 7 ingredients in a large Dutch oven. Bring to a boil over medium heat, stirring until sugar dissolves; add pear slices. Cover, reduce heat, and simmer 10 to 15 minutes or until pear is tender. Let mixture cool slightly. Cover and chill.

Remove pear from cooking liquid. Pour liquid through a wire-mesh strainer into a bowl, discarding cloves and cinnamon stick. Reserve 1½ cups strained liquid; discard remaining liquid.

Place pears in container of an electric blender or food processor; cover and process until smooth. Add sour cream and reserved strained liquid; cover and process until combined. To serve, ladle soup into individual bowls. Sprinkle with cinnamon, if desired. Yield: 6 (¾-cup) servings.

PER SERVING: 142 CALORIES (18% FROM FAT)
FAT 2.9G (SATURATED FAT 1.5G)
PROTEIN 1.2G CARBOHYDRATE 30.4G
CHOLESTEROL 8MG SODIUM 10MG

FRESH RASPBERRY SOUP

7 cups fresh raspberries (about 2 pounds)
¼ cup plus 2 tablespoons sugar
2 tablespoons cornstarch
½ teaspoon grated orange rind
2 cups fresh orange juice
⅔ cup water
⅔ cup plus 2 tablespoons vanilla low-fat yogurt, divided

Place raspberries in container of an electric blender or food processor; cover and process until smooth. Strain raspberries, and discard seeds.

Combine raspberry puree, sugar, and next 4 ingredients in a medium nonaluminum saucepan; stir well. Cook over medium heat, stirring constantly, until mixture comes to a boil. Reduce heat, and simmer, stirring constantly, 1 minute. Remove from heat; let cool. Pour mixture into a large bowl; cover and chill.

To serve, add ⅔ cup yogurt to raspberry mixture, stirring well. Ladle soup into individual bowls; top each with 1 teaspoon yogurt, swirling yogurt to form a design, if desired. Yield: 6 (1-cup) servings.

PER SERVING: 195 CALORIES (6% FROM FAT)
FAT 1.3G (SATURATED FAT 0.3G)
PROTEIN 3.4G CARBOHYDRATE 45.5G
CHOLESTEROL 1MG SODIUM 21MG

STRAWBERRY SOUP

2 cups fresh strawberries, halved
1 tablespoon chopped pecans
1 (6-ounce) carton vanilla nonfat yogurt, divided
2 tablespoons dry red wine
2 teaspoons sugar
Sliced strawberries (optional)

Combine strawberries and pecans in container of an electric blender or food processor; cover and process until smooth, stopping once to scrape down sides. Reserve 1 tablespoon yogurt; add remaining yogurt to strawberry mixture, stirring well. Add wine and sugar; cover and process until blended. Cover and chill.

To serve, ladle soup into individual bowls. Drizzle 1½ teaspoons reserved yogurt over each serving. Garnish with sliced strawberries, if desired. Yield: 2 (1-cup) servings.

PER SERVING: 123 CALORIES (21% FROM FAT)
FAT 2.9G (SATURATED FAT 0.3G)
PROTEIN 5.7G CARBOHYDRATE 17.5G
CHOLESTEROL 2MG SODIUM 67MG

Oniony Vegetable-Beef Soup (recipe on page 45)

HEARTY MEAT FAVORITES

Chock-full of meat and often vegetables, these hot soups and stews are satisfying for lunch or dinner. Along with a loaf of crusty French bread, meaty soups are often sufficient for a full meal. Or you can add a salad and dessert to round out the menu.

Many of these recipes are perfect for busy schedules because they can be put together quickly and then left to simmer. Take a look at page 47 for two especially easy soups made with ground round.

Following the beef recipes are soups and stews made with veal, lamb, and pork. As always, fat-trimming techniques are recommended to cut out every speck of unnecessary fat.

Chinese Hot Pot of Beef

CHINESE HOT POT OF BEEF

2½ pounds beef short ribs
1 tablespoon low-sodium soy sauce
2 teaspoons Chinese five-spice powder
12½ cups water, divided
½ teaspoon black peppercorns
3 medium onions, quartered
3 green onions
2 carrots, scraped and cut into 2-inch pieces
2½ cups sliced fresh mushrooms
1½ cups cubed firm tofu (about ½ pound)
3 tablespoons low-sodium soy sauce
1 teaspoon salt
4 cups cooked Chinese-style noodles
¼ cup thinly sliced green onions
¼ cup chopped fresh cilantro

Combine first 3 ingredients in a 13- x 9- x 2-inch baking pan; toss to coat. Bake at 400° for 30 minutes. Remove ribs from pan, and set aside. Add ½ cup water to pan, and stir to deglaze pan.

Combine pan drippings, ribs, remaining 12 cups water, peppercorns, and next 3 ingredients in a large Dutch oven or stockpot; bring to a boil. Reduce heat, and simmer, uncovered, 2 hours.

Remove ribs from broth, and let cool completely. Remove meat from bones; discard bones, fat, and gristle. Place meat in a bowl; cover and chill. Strain broth through a sieve into a large bowl; discard solids. Cover broth, and chill 12 hours. Skim solidified fat from surface of broth, and discard.

Combine broth, meat, mushrooms, tofu, 3 tablespoons soy sauce, and salt in Dutch oven; bring to a simmer. Cover and cook 10 minutes. Spoon noodles into individual soup bowls. Ladle 2 cups soup into each bowl; sprinkle with 1½ teaspoons each of green onions and cilantro. Yield: 8 (2-cup) servings.

PER SERVING: 232 CALORIES (31% FROM FAT)
FAT 8.1G (SATURATED FAT 2.9G)
PROTEIN 19.5G   CARBOHYDRATE 22.3G
CHOLESTEROL 30MG   SODIUM 581MG

HUNGARIAN VEGETABLE SOUP

1½ pounds lean boneless round steak
    (½ inch thick)
Vegetable cooking spray
1 teaspoon vegetable oil
3 cups chopped onion
3 cloves garlic, minced
5 cups water
2 cups no-salt-added tomato juice
1 (14½-ounce) can no-salt-added whole
    tomatoes, undrained and chopped
3 tablespoons Hungarian paprika
1 tablespoon beef-flavored bouillon granules
1½ teaspoons dried marjoram
¾ teaspoon cracked pepper
1 small dried red chile, seeded and minced
2 cups peeled, cubed potato
1 cup diced carrot

   Trim fat from steak, and cut steak into 1-inch pieces. Set aside.

   Coat a large Dutch oven with cooking spray; add oil. Place over medium-high heat until hot. Add onion and garlic; sauté until tender. Reduce heat to medium. Add steak; cook until browned, stirring frequently. Drain well, and pat dry with paper towels. Wipe drippings from pan with a paper towel.

   Return meat mixture to pan; add water and next 7 ingredients. Bring to a boil; cover, reduce heat, and simmer 1 hour. Add potato and carrot. Cover and simmer 45 minutes or until meat and vegetables are tender. Yield: 14 (1-cup) servings.

PER SERVING: 130 CALORIES (27% FROM FAT)
FAT 3.9G (SATURATED FAT 1.2G)
PROTEIN 12.5G CARBOHYDRATE 11.9G
CHOLESTEROL 31MG SODIUM 243MG

ONIONY VEGETABLE-BEEF SOUP

(pictured on page 42)

½ pound lean boneless top round steak
Vegetable cooking spray
1 teaspoon olive oil
1½ cups thinly sliced onion
1 teaspoon sugar
¾ teaspoon salt
1 tablespoon minced garlic
1½ cups water
2 (14¼-ounce) cans no-salt-added beef broth
1 (14½-ounce) can no-salt-added whole
    tomatoes, undrained and chopped
½ teaspoon dried thyme
½ teaspoon pepper
1 bay leaf
1½ cups coarsely chopped cabbage
1 cup chopped celery
1 cup sliced carrot
1 medium-size yellow squash, cut into 1-inch
    chunks
1 small zucchini, cut into 1-inch chunks

   Trim fat from steak; cut steak into 1-inch pieces. Coat a Dutch oven with cooking spray; place over medium-high heat until hot. Add steak; cook until browned on all sides, stirring frequently. Remove steak from pan; drain and set aside.

   Add oil to pan. Place over medium-high heat until hot. Add onion; sauté 5 minutes or until tender. Reduce heat to medium-low; add sugar and salt. Cook 15 to 20 minutes or until golden, stirring occasionally. Add garlic; cook 1 minute.

   Add steak, water, and next 5 ingredients to onion mixture. Bring to a boil; cover, reduce heat, and simmer 1 hour. Add cabbage and remaining ingredients. Cover and simmer 25 to 30 minutes or until vegetables are tender. Remove and discard bay leaf. Yield: 10 (1-cup) servings.

PER SERVING: 79 CALORIES (18% FROM FAT)
FAT 1.6G (SATURATED FAT 0.4G)
PROTEIN 6.8G CARBOHYDRATE 9.0G
CHOLESTEROL 13MG SODIUM 216MG

Pot-au-Feu with Green Sauce

POT-AU-FEU WITH GREEN SAUCE

2 large onions (about 1 pound)
1 (2-pound) beef brisket
12 cups water
½ teaspoon pepper
¼ teaspoon salt
8 large carrots, scraped and cut into 2-inch
    pieces
5 cloves garlic, halved
4 stalks celery, cut into 2-inch pieces
4 bay leaves
4 large parsley sprigs
3 medium leeks (about 1¾ pounds), trimmed
    and cut in half lengthwise
2 medium turnips (about ½ pound), peeled and
    quartered
Green Sauce

Peel onions, leaving roots intact; cut each onion into 4 wedges. Trim fat from brisket, and thinly slice. Combine brisket, onion, water, and next 9 ingredients in a large Dutch oven; bring to a boil. Reduce heat, and simmer, uncovered, 2 hours or until brisket is tender. Cover and simmer 1 hour. Strain mixture through a cheesecloth-lined colander into a large bowl; discard garlic, bay leaves, parsley, and leeks. Place brisket, onion, carrot, celery, and turnips in a bowl; cover and chill. Cover broth; chill 24 hours.

Remove solidified fat from broth, and discard. Combine broth and brisket mixture in Dutch oven; cook over medium heat until heated. Ladle 1¼ cups broth and one-eighth of meat and vegetables into each bowl; top each with 2 tablespoons Green Sauce. Yield: 8 servings.

GREEN SAUCE

1 cup fresh flat-leaf parsley leaves
⅓ cup fresh lemon juice
2 tablespoons capers
1 tablespoon water
¼ teaspoon pepper
8 pitted green olives
6 green onions, cut into 2-inch pieces
1 canned anchovy fillet or 1 teaspoon anchovy
    paste
1 clove garlic, minced

Combine all ingredients in a food processor; cover and process until smooth. Yield: 1 cup.

PER SERVING: 222 CALORIES (35% FROM FAT)
FAT 8.6G (SATURATED FAT 2.9G)
PROTEIN 20.1G CARBOHYDRATE 16.7G
CHOLESTEROL 56MG SODIUM 473MG

QUICK-AND-EASY VEGETABLE SOUP

This recipe makes a big batch of soup. Enjoy it now, and freeze the remainder for later. Frozen in an air-tight container, the soup will keep up to one month.

1 pound ground round
1¼ cups chopped onion
8 (5½-ounce) cans low-sodium vegetable juice
2 (14½-ounce) cans no-salt-added whole
    tomatoes, undrained and coarsely chopped
1 (14¼-ounce) can no-salt-added beef broth
1 (10-ounce) package frozen chopped okra
1 (10-ounce) package frozen baby lima beans
1 (10-ounce) package frozen whole-kernel
    corn
1 teaspoon coarsely ground pepper
½ teaspoon salt

Cook ground round and onion in a Dutch oven over medium-high heat until beef is browned, stirring until it crumbles. Drain beef mixture, and pat dry with paper towels. Wipe drippings from pan with a paper towel.

Return beef mixture to pan. Stir in vegetable juice and remaining ingredients. Bring to a boil; cover, reduce heat, and simmer 1 hour. Yield: 12 (1½-cup) servings.

PER SERVING: 143 CALORIES (16% FROM FAT)
FAT 2.6G (SATURATED FAT 0.9G)
PROTEIN 11.1G CARBOHYDRATE 21.0G
CHOLESTEROL 22MG SODIUM 238MG

STICK-TO-YOUR-RIBS SOUP

1 pound ground round
5 cups water
4 cups chopped green cabbage (about 1 pound)
3½ cups tomato juice
1 tablespoon dried oregano
1½ teaspoons garlic powder
1 teaspoon salt
1½ teaspoons pepper
¼ teaspoon dried thyme
3 (15-ounce) cans kidney beans, drained
3 (14½-ounce) cans whole tomatoes,
    undrained and chopped
2 (14¼-ounce) cans no-salt-added beef broth
8 ounces angel hair pasta, uncooked

Cook ground round in a large Dutch oven over medium heat until browned, stirring until it crumbles. Drain meat in a colander, and set aside. Wipe drippings from pan with a paper towel.

Return meat to pan. Add water and next 10 ingredients, and bring to a boil. Reduce heat, and simmer, uncovered, 2 hours, stirring occasionally.

Break pasta in half; stir into soup, and cook 5 additional minutes or until pasta is tender. Yield: 13 (1½-cup) servings.

PER SERVING: 163 CALORIES (10% FROM FAT)
FAT 1.9G (SATURATED FAT 0.6G)
PROTEIN 14.7G CARBOHYDRATE 22.8G
CHOLESTEROL 19MG SODIUM 625MG

Island Beef Stew

ISLAND BEEF STEW

3 pounds lean boneless chuck roast, trimmed
3 tablespoons all-purpose flour
1 tablespoon olive oil
2 (14½-ounce) cans no-salt-added whole
   tomatoes, undrained and chopped
3 cups vertically sliced onion
1 teaspoon salt
1¼ teaspoons pepper
2 cups water
⅓ cup molasses
⅓ cup white vinegar
2½ cups thinly sliced carrot (about 1 pound)
½ cup raisins
½ teaspoon ground ginger

Dredge beef in flour. Heat oil in a large Dutch oven; add beef, and cook until browned on all sides. Add tomatoes, onion, salt, and pepper. Combine water, molasses, and vinegar; stir into beef mixture. Cover, reduce heat, and simmer 1 hour and 15 minutes or until beef is tender. Stir in carrot, raisins, and ginger; simmer 30 additional minutes or until carrot is tender.

Remove roast from pan. Separate roast into bite-size pieces; shred with 2 forks. Return shredded roast to pan, and stir. Yield: 9 (1-cup) servings.

PER SERVING: 277 CALORIES (24% FROM FAT)
FAT 7.3G (SATURATED FAT 2.4G)
PROTEIN 26.1G   CARBOHYDRATE 27.3G
CHOLESTEROL 68MG   SODIUM 365MG

BAKED BURGUNDY BEEF STEW

Baking the stew slowly allows the flavors to blend, creating a thick, rich-tasting broth.

2 teaspoons garlic powder
2 teaspoons dried thyme
1 teaspoon pepper
2 pounds lean boneless sirloin steak, cut into
     1-inch pieces
Vegetable cooking spray
3 cups canned no-salt-added beef broth,
     undiluted and divided
2 cups Burgundy or other dry red wine
¼ cup all-purpose flour
3 cups sliced carrot
2 tablespoons no-salt-added tomato paste
1 tablespoon plus 1 teaspoon minced garlic
2 teaspoons minced fresh rosemary
2 cups frozen pearl onions
4 cups small fresh mushrooms

Combine first 3 ingredients, and sprinkle evenly over steak.

Coat a large nonstick skillet with cooking spray; place over medium-high heat until hot. Add steak, and cook until steak is browned on all sides, stirring frequently. Transfer steak to a 4-quart casserole, and set aside.

Add 2¾ cups broth and wine to skillet; cook over high heat, deglazing skillet by scraping particles that cling to bottom.

Combine flour and remaining ¼ cup broth, stirring with a wire whisk until smooth. Reduce heat to medium; add flour mixture to wine mixture, stirring constantly. Cook, stirring constantly, until mixture is thickened. Add carrot, tomato paste, garlic, and rosemary; stir well. Bring to a boil; pour wine mixture over steak. Cover and bake at 350° for 1½ hours, stirring occasionally. Add onions, and bake 30 minutes. Add mushrooms, and bake 30 additional minutes. Yield: 9 (1-cup) servings.

PER SERVING: 214 CALORIES (23% FROM FAT)
FAT 5.5G (SATURATED FAT 1.9G)
PROTEIN 24.2G CARBOHYDRATE 16.2G
CHOLESTEROL 61MG SODIUM 90MG

MOROCCAN BEEF STEW

1 pound lean boneless sirloin steak
Vegetable cooking spray
1⅓ cups chopped onion
3 cloves garlic, minced
1 cup dry red wine
1 cup water
½ cup pitted prunes, halved
¼ cup dried apricots, cut into ¼-inch strips
¼ cup raisins
1½ teaspoons ground cumin
1 teaspoon dried thyme
¼ teaspoon salt
⅛ teaspoon ground red pepper
6 green olives, sliced
1 bay leaf

Trim fat from steak; cut steak into 1-inch cubes, and set aside. Coat a small Dutch oven with cooking spray; place over medium heat until hot. Add steak, and cook until browned on all sides; drain well, and set aside. Wipe drippings from pan with a paper towel.

Recoat pan with cooking spray; place over medium heat until hot. Add onion and garlic; sauté 1 minute. Return steak to pan; add wine and remaining ingredients. Bring to a boil. Cover and reduce heat; simmer 1½ hours or until steak is tender. Discard bay leaf. Yield: 5 (1-cup) servings.

PER SERVING: 230 CALORIES (18% FROM FAT)
FAT 4.6G (SATURATED FAT 1.3G)
PROTEIN 17.1G CARBOHYDRATE 32.3G
CHOLESTEROL 39MG SODIUM 225MG

Flavor Tips

• Boost flavor in homemade stews by adding a splash of red wine to beef or lamb mixtures and sherry to seafood or chicken.
• Save leftover cooking liquid from vegetables to enrich soups and stews.
• Taste the stew before serving, and add additional herbs or other seasonings, if desired.

SOUTHWESTERN BEEF STEW

1 pound lean boneless round steak
Vegetable cooking spray
1 (14½-ounce) can no-salt-added whole
   tomatoes, undrained and chopped
1 cup water
1 cup peeled, cubed potato
1 cup sliced carrot
¾ cup chopped onion
¾ cup light beer
¼ cup chopped sweet red pepper
¼ cup chopped fresh cilantro
2 teaspoons dried oregano
1½ teaspoons chili powder
1 teaspoon beef-flavored bouillon granules
1 jalapeño pepper, seeded and chopped
1 clove garlic, minced
2 tablespoons all-purpose flour
2 tablespoons water

Trim fat from steak; cut steak into 1-inch pieces.
Coat a Dutch oven with cooking spray; place over medium-high heat until hot. Add steak; cook 10 minutes or until steak is browned on all sides. Drain and pat dry with paper towels. Wipe drippings from pan with a paper towel. Return steak to pan; add tomatoes and next 12 ingredients. Bring to a boil. Cover, reduce heat, and simmer 1 hour and 15 minutes or until meat is tender.

Combine flour and 2 tablespoons water, stirring until smooth. Add to stew, and stir well. Cook over medium heat, stirring constantly, until thickened and bubbly. Yield: 6 (1-cup) servings.

PER SERVING: 172 CALORIES (20% FROM FAT)
FAT 3.8G (SATURATED FAT 1.3G)
PROTEIN 17.1G CARBOHYDRATE 17.4G
CHOLESTEROL 39MG SODIUM 225MG

AUTUMN BEEF STEW

1½ pounds lean boneless round steak
   (½ inch thick)
Vegetable cooking spray
1½ cups coarsely chopped onion
1 cup sliced fresh mushrooms
2½ cups water
1 cup cranberry juice cocktail
½ cup dry red wine
1½ teaspoons beef-flavored bouillon granules
½ teaspoon dried rosemary
¼ teaspoon dried thyme
¼ teaspoon ground allspice
¼ teaspoon pepper
2 cups peeled, seeded, and coarsely chopped
   acorn squash
2 cups sliced parsnips
2 tablespoons chopped fresh parsley

Trim fat from steak; cut steak into 1-inch pieces. Coat a large Dutch oven with cooking spray; place over medium-high heat until hot. Add steak; cook until browned on all sides, stirring frequently. Drain and pat dry with paper towels. Wipe drippings from pan with a paper towel.

Coat pan with cooking spray; place over medium-high heat until hot. Add onion and mushrooms; sauté until tender. Add steak, water, and next 7 ingredients, stirring well. Bring to a boil; cover, reduce heat, and simmer 1 hour and 15 minutes. Add squash and parsnips; cover and simmer 40 minutes or until meat and vegetables are tender. Ladle soup into individual bowls. Sprinkle each serving with ¾ teaspoon parsley. Yield: 8 (1-cup) servings.

PER SERVING: 195 CALORIES (26% FROM FAT)
FAT 5.7G (SATURATED FAT 1.9G)
PROTEIN 19.4G CARBOHYDRATE 16.7G
CHOLESTEROL 52MG SODIUM 226MG

Chestnut Beef Stew

CHESTNUT BEEF STEW

1 pound lean beef stew meat
3 tablespoons all-purpose flour
1 tablespoon vegetable oil
1½ cups water
½ teaspoon dried thyme
½ teaspoon pepper
¼ teaspoon dried marjoram
⅛ teaspoon dried sage
6 cloves garlic, peeled
2 (10½-ounce) cans beef broth
2 tablespoons cold water
1 tablespoon all-purpose flour
3 cups (1-inch) peeled, cubed eggplant
2 cups quartered small red potato
1½ cups cooked, shelled, and halved chestnuts
     (about 1½ pounds in shells)
1 (14½-ounce) can no-salt-added stewed
     tomatoes, undrained
Fresh thyme sprigs (optional)

Trim fat from beef. Cut beef into 1-inch cubes. Combine beef and 3 tablespoons flour in a large zip-top plastic bag. Seal bag, and shake well to coat. Heat oil in a large Dutch oven over medium heat. Add beef, and cook 5 minutes, browning on all sides. Add 1½ cups water and next 6 ingredients; bring to a boil. Cover, reduce heat to low, and simmer 1 hour.

Combine cold water and 1 tablespoon flour in a small bowl; stir well. Add flour mixture, eggplant, potato, chestnuts, and tomatoes to beef mixture; bring to a boil. Cover; reduce heat to medium-low. Simmer 30 minutes or until vegetables are tender and stew is thick. Ladle into individual bowls, and garnish with thyme sprigs, if desired. Yield: 6 (1½-cup) servings.

PER SERVING: 328 CALORIES (17% FROM FAT)
FAT 6.3G (SATURATED FAT 1.7G)
PROTEIN 25.4G CARBOHYDRATE 42.4G
CHOLESTEROL 62MG SODIUM 704MG

BEEF AND MUSHROOM STEW

1 pound lean beef stew meat
Vegetable cooking spray
1 cup chopped onion
2 tablespoons all-purpose flour
¼ teaspoon salt
¼ teaspoon pepper
3 cups crimini or button mushrooms (about
    ½ pound), halved
1 cup dry vermouth
1 cup canned low-salt chicken broth, undiluted
3 tablespoons fresh orange juice
1 teaspoon dried basil
½ teaspoon dried thyme
3 cloves garlic, crushed
1 (14½-ounce) can diced tomatoes, undrained
Flat-leaf parsley sprigs (optional)

Trim fat from beef; cut beef into 1-inch cubes. Coat a large nonstick skillet with cooking spray; place over medium-high heat until hot. Add beef and onion; sauté 5 minutes. Combine flour, salt, and pepper; sprinkle over beef mixture, and cook, stirring constantly, 1 minute. Add mushrooms and next 7 ingredients; bring to a boil. Reduce heat, and simmer, uncovered, 40 minutes or until beef is tender, stirring occasionally. Garnish with parsley, if desired. Yield: 4 (1½-cup) servings.

Note: Substitute 1 cup chicken broth for vermouth, if desired.

PER SERVING: 291 CALORIES (29% FROM FAT)
FAT 9.4G (SATURATED FAT 3.3G)
PROTEIN 31.9G   CARBOHYDRATE 19.1G
CHOLESTEROL 86MG   SODIUM 608MG

Beef and Mushroom Stew

MEATBALL AND MACARONI STEW

½ English muffin, cut into ½-inch pieces
3 tablespoons skim milk
½ pound ground round
¼ cup grated Parmesan cheese
¼ cup chopped fresh parsley
⅛ teaspoon pepper
⅛ teaspoon salt
1 egg white
Vegetable cooking spray
2 cups chopped onion
2 cloves garlic, minced
1½ teaspoons dried basil
1 teaspoon dried oregano
1 (28-ounce) can Italian-style tomatoes, undrained and chopped
1 (14¼-ounce) can no-salt-added chicken broth
⅔ cup dry red wine
2 teaspoons sugar
½ teaspoon salt
1 bay leaf
3 cups cooked large elbow macaroni (cooked without salt or fat)

Combine muffin and milk in a large bowl; stir well, and let stand 5 minutes or until liquid is absorbed. Add ground round and next 5 ingredients; stir well. Shape mixture into 18 (1-inch) balls; cover and set aside.

Coat a Dutch oven with cooking spray; place over medium heat until hot. Add onion and garlic; sauté 10 minutes or until tender. Add basil and oregano; cook 1 minute. Stir in tomatoes and next 5 ingredients; bring to a boil. Add meatballs; reduce heat, and simmer, uncovered, 15 minutes or until done. Discard bay leaf. Stir in macaroni, and cook until heated. Yield: 8 (1-cup) servings.

Note: Substitute ⅔ cup no-salt-added chicken broth for wine, if desired.

PER SERVING: 195 CALORIES (16% FROM FAT)
FAT 3.4G (SATURATED FAT 1.1G)
PROTEIN 12.9G CARBOHYDRATE 28.2G
CHOLESTEROL 19MG SODIUM 493MG

HEARTY HAMBURGER STEW

Vegetable cooking spray
1 pound ground round
1 cup chopped onion
3 cups water
1 (14½-ounce) can no-salt-added whole tomatoes, undrained and chopped
½ cup chopped celery
2 teaspoons beef-flavored bouillon granules
2 teaspoons low-sodium Worcestershire sauce
⅛ teaspoon pepper
1 bay leaf
1 (10-ounce) package frozen baby lima beans
1 (8¾-ounce) can no-salt-added whole-kernel corn, drained
4 ounces small macaroni shells, uncooked

Coat a Dutch oven with cooking spray; place over medium heat until hot. Add ground round and onion; cook until meat is browned, stirring until it crumbles. Drain meat mixture; pat dry with paper towels. Wipe drippings from pan with a paper towel.

Return meat mixture to pan; add water and next 6 ingredients, stirring well. Bring to a boil; cover, reduce heat, and simmer 30 minutes.

Add lima beans, corn, and macaroni; bring to a boil. Reduce heat, and simmer, uncovered, 20 minutes, stirring occasionally. Remove and discard bay leaf. Yield: 9 (1-cup) servings.

PER SERVING: 191 CALORIES (16% FROM FAT)
FAT 3.4G (SATURATED FAT 1.0G)
PROTEIN 15.2G CARBOHYDRATE 24.6G
CHOLESTEROL 28MG SODIUM 309MG

Veal Stew with Cilantro-Chile Sauce

VEAL STEW WITH CILANTRO-CHILE SAUCE

1 (2-pound) boneless veal leg roast
3½ cups canned low-salt chicken broth, undiluted
1 cup sliced carrot
¾ cup sliced celery
½ cup thinly sliced green onions
⅓ cup thinly sliced seeded jalapeño pepper
⅓ cup fresh cilantro leaves
6 cloves garlic
1 bay leaf
½ cup unsweetened orange juice
¼ cup fresh lemon juice
½ teaspoon salt
¼ cup thinly sliced green onions
2 tablespoons minced fresh cilantro

Trim fat from roast. Combine roast, broth, and next 7 ingredients in a large Dutch oven; bring to a boil. Remove from heat; cover and bake at 325° for 1 hour and 15 minutes or until roast is tender. Remove roast from pan, reserving cooking liquid and vegetables; let roast stand 10 minutes. Separate roast into bite-size pieces, and shred; set aside.

Remove bay leaf from cooking liquid, and discard. Place cooking liquid and vegetables in container of an electric blender or food processor; cover and process until smooth. Return puree to pan. Add fruit juices; bring to a boil, and cook 18 minutes or until reduced to 2 cups. Return shredded roast to pan; stir in salt. Cook over medium heat until thoroughly heated. Ladle stew into individual bowls, and top each with 1 tablespoon green onions and 1½ teaspoons minced cilantro. Serve with flour tortillas. Yield: 4 (1-cup) servings.

PER SERVING: 323 CALORIES (16% FROM FAT)
FAT 5.6G (SATURATED FAT 1.3G)
PROTEIN 52.1G   CARBOHYDRATE 14.8G
CHOLESTEROL 177MG   SODIUM 544MG

VEAL STEW WITH SAGE

2½ tablespoons all-purpose flour
⅛ teaspoon pepper
1 pound veal sirloin tip roast, cut into ½-inch
    cubes
Vegetable cooking spray
1 cup coarsely chopped onion
⅓ cup thinly sliced celery
½ cup dry white wine
1 (14½-ounce) can plum tomatoes, undrained
    and chopped
2 teaspoons minced fresh sage
Dash of salt
½ teaspoon grated lemon rind
Fresh sage leaves (optional)

Combine flour and pepper in a large zip-top plastic bag. Add veal; seal bag, and shake to coat. Set veal mixture aside.

Coat a large nonstick saucepan with cooking spray; place over medium-high heat until hot. Add onion and celery. Cover, reduce heat, and simmer 10 minutes or until tender. (Do not brown.) Add veal; sauté over medium-high heat until veal is browned.

Add wine to veal mixture; bring to a boil. Cook 5 minutes, stirring occasionally. Stir in tomatoes, minced sage, and salt. Cover, reduce heat, and simmer 30 minutes. Stir in lemon rind. Cook, uncovered, 10 additional minutes. Garnish with fresh sage leaves, if desired. Yield: 3 (1-cup) servings.

PER SERVING: 241 CALORIES (12% FROM FAT)
FAT 3.3G (SATURATED FAT 0.9G)
PROTEIN 35.0G CARBOHYDRATE 16.9G
CHOLESTEROL 118MG SODIUM 386MG

BAKED SPLIT PEA SOUP

1 pound lean boneless lamb
4 cups water
1½ cups dried split peas
1 cup diced onion
⅔ cup chopped carrot
1 teaspoon dried thyme
1 teaspoon minced garlic
¼ teaspoon salt
¼ teaspoon ground white pepper
1 (14½-ounce) can no-salt-added whole
    tomatoes, undrained and chopped

Trim fat from lamb; cut lamb into 1-inch cubes. Combine lamb, water, and next 7 ingredients in a 3-quart casserole. Cover and bake at 325° for 1 hour and 35 minutes. Stir in tomatoes. Cover and bake 10 additional minutes or until peas are tender. Yield: 9 (1-cup) servings.

PER SERVING: 209 CALORIES (12% FROM FAT)
FAT 2.8G (SATURATED FAT 0.9G)
PROTEIN 20.0G CARBOHYDRATE 26.9G
CHOLESTEROL 32MG SODIUM 112MG

Menu Planner

Health advisory groups recommend that at least 50 percent of our daily calories come from carbohydrates, so you can feel free to round out most soup or stew meals with bread.

French or Italian bread, bagels, breadsticks, toasted pita bread, or warm flour tortillas are good choices because they are all naturally low in fat. And with lighter soups, crackers are always an option.

GREEK LAMB AND ARTICHOKE SOUP

10 cups water
3 medium leeks, trimmed and halved
2 bay leaves
1 medium onion, peeled and halved
1 fennel bulb, quartered
1½ pounds lean ground lamb
1 cup soft breadcrumbs
½ cup tomato juice
2 teaspoons dried dillweed
½ teaspoon salt
½ teaspoon ground oregano
½ teaspoon pepper
2 cloves garlic, minced
2 cups cooked rice (cooked without salt or fat)
⅓ cup fresh lemon juice
2 (15-ounce) cans cannellini beans or other white beans, drained
2 (14-ounce) cans quartered artichoke hearts, drained
2 eggs

Combine first 5 ingredients in a Dutch oven; bring to a boil. Partially cover, reduce heat, and simmer 45 minutes. Remove from heat, and set aside.

Combine lamb and next 7 ingredients in a bowl, and stir well. Shape mixture into 24 (1¼-inch) meatballs. Place a large nonstick skillet over medium-high heat until hot. Add meatballs, and cook 10 minutes or until browned, stirring frequently. Remove from skillet, and pat dry with paper towels; set aside, and keep warm.

Strain stock through a colander into a large bowl; discard solids. Reserve 2 cups stock; set aside. Return remaining stock to pan, and bring to a boil; add meatballs, rice, lemon juice, beans, and artichokes. Return to a boil, and reduce heat to low.

Place eggs in a bowl; stir well. Gradually add reserved 2 cups stock, stirring constantly with a wire whisk. Slowly drizzle egg mixture into soup, stirring constantly. Yield: 14 (1-cup) servings.

PER SERVING: 202 CALORIES (20% FROM FAT)
FAT 4.6G (SATURATED FAT 1.6G)
PROTEIN 17.1G CARBOHYDRATE 23.2G
CHOLESTEROL 65MG SODIUM 387MG

SPICY LAMB STEW

Vegetable cooking spray
1 pound lean boneless lamb, cut into ¾-inch cubes
1 teaspoon ground coriander
1 teaspoon ground cumin
¼ teaspoon salt
⅛ teaspoon ground red pepper
⅛ teaspoon black pepper
1 cup finely chopped onion
2 teaspoons peeled, minced gingerroot
1 large clove garlic, minced
2 cups canned no-salt-added beef broth, undiluted
1 cup peeled, chopped tomato
1 cup peeled, cubed red potato
2 cups chopped fresh spinach leaves
¼ cup plain low-fat yogurt

Coat a large Dutch oven with cooking spray, and place over medium-high heat until hot. Add lamb, and cook 3 minutes or until browned, stirring frequently. Drain well. Combine lamb, coriander, cumin, salt, and red and black pepper in a bowl; toss well, and set aside. Wipe drippings from pan with a paper towel.

Recoat pan with cooking spray, and place over medium heat until hot. Add onion, gingerroot, and garlic; sauté 3 minutes. Return lamb mixture to pan; stir-fry 2 minutes. Add broth and tomato; stir well, and bring to a boil.

Cover, reduce heat, and simmer 1 hour and 15 minutes, stirring occasionally. Add cubed potato; cover and simmer 20 minutes. Stir in chopped spinach; cover and simmer 5 additional minutes. Ladle stew into individual bowls; top each with 1 tablespoon yogurt. Yield: 4 (1-cup) servings.

PER SERVING: 271 CALORIES (31% FROM FAT)
FAT 9.2G (SATURATED FAT 3.2G)
PROTEIN 29.1G CARBOHYDRATE 16.2G
CHOLESTEROL 82MG SODIUM 263MG

Spicy Lamb Stew

Lamb and Lentil Stew

1 cup plain low-fat yogurt
Vegetable cooking spray
1 teaspoon olive oil
¼ cup chopped onion
2 cloves garlic, minced
¾ pound lean boneless leg of lamb, cut into
    bite-size pieces
2 cups water
1½ cups canned no-salt-added beef broth,
    undiluted and divided
1 cup dried lentils
2 teaspoons ground cumin
1 teaspoon ground coriander
½ teaspoon salt
½ teaspoon pepper
1½ cups peeled, cubed acorn squash (about
    ½ pound)
1 teaspoon cornstarch

Spoon yogurt onto several layers of heavy-duty paper towels, and spread to ½-inch thickness. Cover with additional paper towels, and let stand 5 minutes. Scrape into a bowl, using a rubber spatula, and set aside.

Coat a large Dutch oven with cooking spray; add oil, and place over medium heat until hot. Add onion and garlic, and sauté 2 minutes or until tender. Add lamb, and cook 5 minutes or until browned on all sides, stirring frequently. Add water, 1 cup beef broth, lentils, and next 4 ingredients. Bring mixture to a boil; cover, reduce heat, and simmer 15 minutes. Add cubed acorn squash, and simmer 30 additional minutes or until lamb is tender.

Combine cornstarch and remaining ½ cup beef broth; add to lamb mixture, stirring well. Bring mixture to a boil, and cook 1 minute. Ladle stew into individual bowls, and top each with 1 table-spoon yogurt. Yield: 5 (1-cup) servings.

PER SERVING: 290 CALORIES (17% FROM FAT)
FAT 5.4G (SATURATED FAT 1.8G)
PROTEIN 28.0G CARBOHYDRATE 32.6G
CHOLESTEROL 46MG SODIUM 318MG

Irish Stew

1 pound lean boneless leg of lamb
1 cup peeled, cubed red potato (about ½
    pound)
1 cup thinly sliced onion
1 cup (¼-inch) sliced carrot
½ cup (½-inch) sliced celery
1 cup water
½ teaspoon salt
½ teaspoon dried thyme
½ teaspoon lemon juice
2 tablespoons all-purpose flour
1 tablespoon chopped fresh parsley

Trim fat from lamb, and cut lamb into 1-inch cubes; set aside.

Combine potato, onion, carrot, celery, water, salt, thyme, and lemon juice in a 2½-quart casserole; stir well. Cover and microwave at HIGH 10 to 13 minutes or until vegetables are tender, stirring after 6 minutes. Stir in lamb; microwave at MEDIUM-HIGH (70% power) 3 minutes.

Place ¼ cup cooking liquid in a small bowl. Add flour; stir well with a wire whisk. Add flour mixture to lamb mixture; microwave at MEDIUM-HIGH 3 minutes or until liquid is slightly thickened, stirring after 1½ minutes. Ladle into individual bowls, and sprinkle with parsley. Yield: 4 (1-cup) servings.

PER SERVING: 227 CALORIES (21% FROM FAT)
FAT 5.3G (SATURATED FAT 1.9G)
PROTEIN 25.7G CARBOHYDRATE 18.4G
CHOLESTEROL 73MG SODIUM 391MG

Sausage-Kraut Soup

SAUSAGE-KRAUT SOUP

2 cups dried baby lima beans
½ pound bulk pork sausage
6 cups water
2 cups diced red potato
2 cups refrigerated sauerkraut, drained
1 cup thinly sliced carrot
1 cup diced onion
1 cup chopped broccoli flowerets
½ teaspoon dried summer savory
¼ teaspoon dried thyme
¼ teaspoon dried rosemary
¼ teaspoon pepper
2 cloves garlic, minced
1 (15-ounce) can chick-peas (garbanzo beans),
   drained
1 (10¾-ounce) can reduced-fat, reduced-sodium
   condensed tomato soup, undiluted

Sort and wash beans; place in a large Dutch oven. Cover with water to depth of 2 inches above beans, and bring to a boil; cook 2 minutes. Remove from heat; cover and let stand 1 hour. Drain beans in a colander; set aside.

Cook sausage in pan over medium heat until browned, stirring to crumble. Drain sausage well. Wipe drippings from pan with a paper towel. Return sausage to pan. Stir in beans, water, and next 11 ingredients; bring to a boil. Cover, reduce heat, and simmer 1 hour. Stir in tomato soup; cover and simmer 30 additional minutes. Yield: 10 (1⅓-cup) servings.

PER SERVING: 211 CALORIES (31% FROM FAT)
FAT 7.2G (SATURATED FAT 2.2G)
PROTEIN 10.3G   CARBOHYDRATE 27.2G
CHOLESTEROL 18MG   SODIUM 541MG

PORK-PEPPER SOUP

1 pound lean boneless pork loin (½ inch thick)
Vegetable cooking spray
1 cup chopped onion
2 cloves garlic, minced
1 jalapeño pepper, seeded and sliced
1 cup sliced carrot
2 cups canned low-sodium chicken broth, undiluted
1 cup water
¼ cup chopped fresh parsley
2 tablespoons low-sodium soy sauce
½ teaspoon dried basil
¼ teaspoon dried thyme
¼ teaspoon pepper
1 small green pepper, cut into thin strips
1 small sweet red pepper, cut into thin strips
1 small sweet yellow pepper, cut into thin strips

Trim fat from pork; cut pork into ½-inch cubes. Coat a large Dutch oven with cooking spray; place over medium heat until hot. Add pork, and cook until pork is browned on all sides, stirring frequently. Drain and pat dry with paper towels. Wipe drippings from pan with a paper towel.

Recoat pan with cooking spray; place over medium-high heat until hot. Add onion, garlic, and jalapeño pepper; sauté until tender. Add pork, carrot, and next 7 ingredients. Bring mixture to a boil; cover, reduce heat, and simmer 30 minutes or until pork is tender. Add pepper strips; cover and cook 10 additional minutes or until pepper is tender. Yield: 6 (1-cup) servings.

PER SERVING: 138 CALORIES (33% FROM FAT)
FAT 5.0G (SATURATED FAT 1.4G)
PROTEIN 14.2G   CARBOHYDRATE 9.4G
CHOLESTEROL 34MG   SODIUM 235MG

Pork-Pepper Soup

HARVEST CABBAGE SOUP

Vegetable cooking spray
3 cups shredded cabbage
2½ cups peeled, chopped Rome apple
1 cup diced carrot
½ cup diced green pepper
1 clove garlic, minced
4 cups water
2 cups unsweetened apple juice
2 teaspoons beef-flavored bouillon granules
2 cups cooked egg noodles (cooked without salt or fat)
1½ cups diced cooked lean pork loin
½ teaspoon caraway seeds
½ cup (2 ounces) shredded reduced-fat Swiss cheese
3 tablespoons minced fresh parsley

Coat a large Dutch oven with cooking spray; place over medium-high heat until hot. Add cabbage and next 4 ingredients; sauté 5 minutes or until cabbage begins to wilt. Stir in water, apple juice, and bouillon granules. Bring to a boil. Add noodles, pork, and caraway seeds. Reduce heat; simmer 10 minutes or until thoroughly heated. Ladle soup into bowls; sprinkle with cheese and parsley. Yield: 9 (1-cup) servings.

PER SERVING: 186 CALORIES (23% FROM FAT)
FAT 4.7G (SATURATED FAT 1.6G)
PROTEIN 12.0G CARBOHYDRATE 24.3G
CHOLESTEROL 39MG SODIUM 251MG

FYI

To keep parsley and cilantro fresh, place the bunches, stem down, in a small amount of water in a glass jar. Cover the leaves with a plastic bag, and refrigerate up to one week, changing the water every two days. For longer storage, wash, dry, and chop the leaves, and place in a heavy-duty, zip-top plastic freezer bag. Seal the bag, and freeze.

PORK STEW WITH SWEET POTATOES AND CORN

1½ pounds lean boneless pork loin
1 tablespoon olive oil
2 cups quartered mushrooms
1½ cups thinly sliced leeks
2 cups julienne-sliced carrot
1 cup canned low-salt chicken broth, undiluted
2 teaspoons poultry seasoning
½ teaspoon salt
½ teaspoon coarsely ground pepper
2 (14½-ounce) cans no-salt-added whole tomatoes, undrained and chopped
2 bay leaves
3½ cups chopped sweet potato (about 1 pound)
1 (10-ounce) package frozen whole-kernel corn
2 cups coarsely chopped spinach

Trim fat from pork; cut pork into 1-inch cubes. Heat oil in a large Dutch oven over medium-high heat. Add pork, mushrooms, and leeks; sauté 10 minutes or until browned.

Stir in carrot and next 6 ingredients; bring mixture to a boil. Cover, reduce heat, and simmer 1 hour or until pork is tender. Add sweet potato and corn; cover and simmer 20 minutes or until sweet potato is tender. Add spinach; cover and simmer 2 minutes. Discard bay leaves. Yield: 6 (1¾-cup) servings.

PER SERVING: 394 CALORIES (27% FROM FAT)
FAT 12.0G (SATURATED FAT 3.4G)
PROTEIN 29.4G CARBOHYDRATE 44.7G
CHOLESTEROL 68MG SODIUM 344MG

PORK AND BLACK BEAN STEW

2 cups dried black beans
1 pound lean boneless pork loin
Vegetable cooking spray
2 teaspoons vegetable oil, divided
2 cups chopped onion
2 cups chopped cabbage
1 cup chopped celery
1 tablespoon minced garlic
1 jalapeño pepper, seeded and minced
2 tablespoons ground cumin
2 teaspoons paprika
1 teaspoon dried crushed red pepper
2 cups water
2 (14¼-ounce) cans no-salt-added chicken
    broth
2 (14½-ounce) cans no-salt-added whole
    tomatoes, undrained and chopped
¾ teaspoon salt
½ cup plus 1 tablespoon chopped green onions

Sort and wash beans; place beans in a large Dutch oven. Cover with water to depth of 2 inches above beans; let soak overnight. Drain beans, and set aside.

Trim fat from pork; cut pork into 1-inch cubes. Coat Dutch oven with cooking spray; add 1 teaspoon oil. Place over medium-high heat until hot. Add pork, and cook until browned on all sides, stirring frequently. Remove pork from Dutch oven; set aside.

Add remaining 1 teaspoon oil to pan. Add 2 cups onion and next 4 ingredients; sauté until tender. Stir in cumin, paprika, and pepper; sauté 1 minute.

Add beans, pork, water, and broth to onion mixture. Bring to a boil; cover, reduce heat, and simmer 1 hour. Add tomatoes and salt; cover and cook 1 hour or until beans are tender. Ladle stew into individual bowls; sprinkle each with 1 tablespoon green onions. Yield: 9 (1½-cup) servings.

PER SERVING: 291 CALORIES (19% FROM FAT)
FAT 6.1G (SATURATED FAT 1.7G)
PROTEIN 21.9G CARBOHYDRATE 38.2G
CHOLESTEROL 30MG SODIUM 265MG

PORK AND SQUASH STEW

1 pound pork shoulder
3 tablespoons all-purpose flour
½ teaspoon salt
¼ teaspoon pepper
1 tablespoon vegetable oil, divided
3 cups coarsely chopped onion
2¼ cups sliced carrot
½ teaspoon dried rosemary, crushed
1 (12-ounce) can beer
2 cups peeled, cubed butternut squash (about
    1 pound)
1 tablespoon chopped fresh parsley

Trim fat from pork; cut pork into ¾-inch cubes, and set aside. Combine flour, salt, and pepper in a large heavy-duty, zip-top plastic bag. Add pork to bag; seal bag, and shake to coat.

Heat 2 teaspoons oil in a large nonstick skillet over medium-high heat; add pork, and cook until browned on all sides. Remove pork from skillet, and set aside. Add remaining 1 teaspoon oil to skillet. Add onion and carrot, and sauté 5 minutes or until onion is tender.

Return pork to skillet; add rosemary and beer, and bring to a boil. Cover, reduce heat, and simmer 30 minutes. Add squash; cover and simmer 25 additional minutes or until squash is tender. Ladle into individual bowls, and sprinkle each serving with ½ teaspoon parsley. Yield: 6 (1⅓-cup) servings.

Note: The stew can be frozen in an airtight freezer container. Thaw in the refrigerator.

PER SERVING: 238 CALORIES (32% FROM FAT)
FAT 8.5G (SATURATED FAT 2.5G)
PROTEIN 17.2G CARBOHYDRATE 24.0G
CHOLESTEROL 51MG SODIUM 277MG

Pork and Squash Stew

Chunky Chicken-Potato Soup (recipe on page 72)

PLEASING POULTRY

*C*hicken soup may or may not cure the sniffles, but it certainly offers a lot of comfort. The mere fragrance of a simmering pot of Herbed Chicken Minestrone (page 68) lets you know a little tender-loving care is on the way.

You may want to stock up on a few basic ingredients so that you can stir up a batch of chicken soup in a hurry. Keep canned low-sodium chicken broth and frozen skinned, boned chicken breasts on hand as well as noodles, rice, and fresh, frozen, or canned vegetables.

Most of the recipes in this chapter call for chicken broth. If you want to make the broth from scratch, turn to page 9 for the recipe.

CHICKEN AND BLACK BEAN SOUP

¾ cup dried black beans
2 (14¼-ounce) cans no-salt-added chicken broth
2 cups water
1 teaspoon dried oregano
½ teaspoon ground cumin
Vegetable cooking spray
1 cup chopped purple onion
¾ cup chopped green pepper
¾ cup chopped sweet red pepper
2 cloves garlic, minced
2¼ cups peeled, seeded, and chopped tomato
2 cups chopped cooked chicken breast
1 cup frozen whole-kernel corn, thawed
¼ cup dry sherry
1 teaspoon chicken-flavored bouillon granules

Sort and wash beans; place beans in a large Dutch oven. Cover with water to depth of 2 inches above beans; let soak overnight. Drain beans. Combine beans, broth, 2 cups water, oregano, and cumin in pan; bring to a boil. Cover, reduce heat, and simmer 1 hour or until beans are tender, stirring occasionally.

Coat a large nonstick skillet with cooking spray; place over medium-high heat until hot. Add onion, peppers, and garlic; sauté until tender. Add onion mixture, tomato, and remaining 4 ingredients to bean mixture. Cover, reduce heat, and simmer 30 minutes or until vegetables are tender. Yield: 10 (1-cup) servings.

PER SERVING: 160 CALORIES (17% FROM FAT)
FAT 3.0G (SATURATED FAT 0.7G)
PROTEIN 15.4G   CARBOHYDRATE 18.4G
CHOLESTEROL 28MG   SODIUM 158MG

CHICKEN-CRABMEAT PEPPERPOT

4 (4-ounce) skinned, boned chicken breast halves
5 (10½-ounce) cans low-sodium chicken broth
1 cup chopped onion
1 teaspoon minced garlic
3 cups fresh corn cut from cob (about 5 ears)
½ pound fresh lump crabmeat, drained
1 medium-size sweet red pepper, cut into 1-inch pieces
1 medium-size green pepper, cut into 1-inch pieces
½ cup chopped green onions
½ cup chopped fresh cilantro
1 teaspoon coarsely ground pepper
¼ teaspoon salt

Combine chicken and next 3 ingredients in a large Dutch oven. Bring to a boil; cover, reduce heat, and simmer 20 minutes or until chicken is tender. Remove chicken from broth, reserving broth. Let chicken cool slightly. Shred chicken.

Skim fat from broth; add shredded chicken and corn to broth. Bring to a boil; cover, reduce heat, and simmer 10 minutes. Stir in crabmeat and remaining ingredients; cover and cook 10 minutes or until vegetables are tender. Yield: 11 (1-cup) servings.

PER SERVING: 143 CALORIES (19% FROM FAT)
FAT 3.0G (SATURATED FAT 0.8G)
PROTEIN 16.5G   CARBOHYDRATE 13.8G
CHOLESTEROL 46MG   SODIUM 184MG

Chicken-Crabmeat Pepperpot

CHICKEN AND CORN SOUP

12 cups water
1 cup sliced onion
1 cup coarsely chopped celery
1 pound chicken breast halves
½ pound chicken thighs
½ pound chicken drumsticks
3 cups frozen whole-kernel corn, thawed
4 ounces medium egg noodles, uncooked
¾ teaspoon salt
½ teaspoon pepper
¼ teaspoon threads of saffron
1 egg, lightly beaten
2 tablespoons chopped fresh parsley

Combine first 6 ingredients in a large Dutch oven; bring to a boil. Reduce heat, and simmer, uncovered, 1 hour or until chicken is tender. Remove from heat.

Remove chicken pieces from broth; let cool. Remove skin from chicken, and remove chicken from bones; discard skin and bones. Shred meat into bite-size pieces; cover and chill.

Strain broth through a sieve into a large bowl, reserving 8 cups; discard solids. Cover and chill broth 8 hours. Skim solidified fat from surface of broth, and discard.

Combine broth and chicken in Dutch oven, and bring to a boil. Stir in corn and next 4 ingredients; bring to a boil. Reduce heat, and simmer, uncovered, 10 minutes or until noodles are done. Remove soup from heat.

Slowly pour beaten egg into hot soup, stirring constantly. (The egg will form lacy strands as it cooks.) Ladle into individual bowls; sprinkle with fresh parsley. Yield: 10 (1-cup) servings.

PER SERVING: 171 CALORIES (22% FROM FAT)
FAT 4.2G (SATURATED FAT 1.1G)
PROTEIN 14.5G CARBOHYDRATE 19.9G
CHOLESTEROL 66MG SODIUM 228MG

HERBED CHICKEN MINESTRONE

Vegetable cooking spray
3 (4-ounce) skinned, boned chicken breast halves, cut into ½-inch cubes
1 teaspoon olive oil
1 cup chopped onion
2 cloves garlic, minced
Fresh Herb Stock
2 (8-ounce) cans no-salt-added tomato sauce
1 cup diced zucchini
½ cup chopped celery
½ cup diced carrot
¼ cup minced fresh parsley
1 tablespoon minced fresh basil
¼ teaspoon dried thyme
¼ teaspoon cracked pepper
2 cups peeled, seeded, and diced tomato
½ cup orzo, uncooked

Coat a Dutch oven with cooking spray; place over medium-high heat until hot. Add chicken; sauté 3 minutes or until lightly browned. Remove chicken from pan; pat dry with paper towels. Wipe drippings from pan with a paper towel.

Add oil, onion, and garlic to pan; sauté until tender. Stir in chicken, Fresh Herb Stock, and next 8 ingredients. Bring to a boil; cover, reduce heat, and simmer 15 minutes. Add tomato and orzo. Return to a boil; cover, reduce heat, and simmer 50 minutes to 1 hour or until soup is thickened. Yield: 9 (1-cup) servings.

FRESH HERB STOCK
4 cups water
1 cup no-salt-added tomato juice
¼ cup chopped onion
¼ cup minced fresh parsley
¼ cup minced fresh basil
2 tablespoons minced fresh thyme
2 tablespoons minced fresh oregano
2 tablespoons minced fresh chives
¼ teaspoon salt
1 medium potato, peeled and chopped
1 clove garlic, minced
5 white peppercorns, crushed

Combine all ingredients in a large saucepan. Bring to a boil; cover, reduce heat, and simmer 30 minutes. Remove from heat, and let cool to room temperature. Strain broth through a double layer of cheesecloth. Yield: 4 cups.

PER SERVING: 145 CALORIES (12% FROM FAT)
FAT 2.0G (SATURATED FAT 0.4G)
PROTEIN 11.9G CARBOHYDRATE 20.4G
CHOLESTEROL 23MG SODIUM 116MG

CHINESE NOODLE SOUP

2¼ cups canned low-sodium chicken broth, undiluted
2 tablespoons julienne-sliced carrot
2 tablespoons sliced water chestnuts
2 tablespoons sliced fresh mushrooms
¼ teaspoon peeled, minced gingerroot
1 ounce vermicelli, uncooked
½ cup shredded cooked chicken breast
8 unpeeled medium-size fresh shrimp
½ cup fresh snow pea pods, trimmed
1 tablespoon low-sodium soy sauce
1 tablespoon sliced green onions

Bring chicken broth to a boil in a medium saucepan. Add carrot and next 3 ingredients; cook, uncovered, 2 minutes.

Break vermicelli into pieces, add vermicelli and chicken to broth mixture. Cook over medium heat 5 minutes, stirring occasionally.

Peel and devein shrimp; chop shrimp. Add shrimp and snow peas to broth mixture. Cook 2 to 3 minutes or until shrimp turn pink. Stir in soy sauce.

To serve, ladle soup into individual bowls, and sprinkle evenly with green onions. Yield: 2 servings.

PER SERVING: 245 CALORIES (16% FROM FAT)
FAT 4.3G (SATURATED FAT 0.6G)
PROTEIN 26.8G CARBOHYDRATE 23.1G
CHOLESTEROL 98MG SODIUM 385MG

CHICKEN NOODLE SOUP WITH HERBS

Make double batches of the broth and freeze it for later use.

13 cups water
3¾ pounds chicken pieces, skinned
1 tablespoon black peppercorns
1 teaspoon dried basil
1 teaspoon dried oregano
3 medium parsnips or carrots, each scraped and quartered
3 cloves garlic, each halved
2 medium leeks or onions, each trimmed and quartered
2 stalks celery, each quartered
2 cups sliced carrot
¾ teaspoon salt
⅛ teaspoon pepper
1½ cups fine egg noodles, uncooked

Combine first 9 ingredients in an 8-quart Dutch oven or stockpot; bring to a boil. Reduce heat to medium, and cook, uncovered, 1 hour. Remove from heat.

Remove chicken pieces from broth; place chicken in a bowl, and chill 15 minutes. Strain broth through a sieve into a large bowl, and discard solids.

Remove chicken from bones; shred meat into bite-size pieces. Discard bones. Return broth to pan. Add chicken, sliced carrot, salt, and pepper; bring to a boil. Partially cover, reduce heat to medium, and cook 10 minutes. Add noodles; partially cover, and cook 10 additional minutes. Yield: 7 (1½-cup) servings.

PER SERVING: 227 CALORIES (18% FROM FAT)
FAT 4.6G (SATURATED FAT 1.2G)
PROTEIN 33.3G CARBOHYDRATE 11.1G
CHOLESTEROL 111MG SODIUM 374MG

COCK-A-LEEKIE SOUP

Chicken and leeks are the main ingredients in this classic Scottish soup.

Vegetable cooking spray
1 teaspoon vegetable oil
8 cups thinly sliced leeks (about 5 leeks)
6 cups water
1½ cups thinly sliced celery
¾ cup diced carrot
3 tablespoons chopped fresh parsley
2 teaspoons beef-flavored bouillon granules
½ teaspoon pepper
1 bay leaf
1½ cups diced cooked chicken breast

Coat a Dutch oven with cooking spray; add oil. Place over medium-high heat until hot. Add leeks, and sauté until tender. Stir in water and next 6 ingredients; stir well. Bring mixture to a boil; cover, reduce heat, and simmer 40 minutes or until vegetables are tender.

Add chicken to vegetable mixture, stirring well. Cover and cook until thoroughly heated. Remove and discard bay leaf. Yield: 8 (1-cup) servings.

PER SERVING: 124 CALORIES (18% FROM FAT)
FAT 2.5G (SATURATED FAT 0.5G)
PROTEIN 12.5G CARBOHYDRATE 13.1G
CHOLESTEROL 30MG SODIUM 298MG

CREAMY CHICKEN, LEEK, AND MUSHROOM SOUP

Vegetable cooking spray
3 cups chopped leeks (about 3 medium)
2¼ pounds chicken thighs, skinned, boned, and cut into bite-size pieces
3 cloves garlic, minced
4 cups quartered fresh mushrooms (about 12 ounces)
3 cups canned no-salt-added chicken broth, undiluted
⅓ cup dry white wine
½ cup all-purpose flour
2½ cups 2% low-fat milk
2 tablespoons dry sherry
½ teaspoon salt
¼ teaspoon pepper

Coat a large Dutch oven with cooking spray; place over medium-high heat until hot. Add leeks, chicken, and garlic, and sauté 10 minutes. Add mushrooms, and sauté 5 minutes. Add broth and wine; bring to a boil. Reduce heat, and simmer, uncovered, 10 minutes.

Place flour in a small bowl. Gradually add milk, stirring with a wire whisk until well blended; add to soup. Cook over medium heat, stirring constantly, 10 minutes or until thickened. Stir in sherry, salt, and pepper. Yield: 6 (1½-cup) servings.

PER SERVING: 275 CALORIES (22% FROM FAT)
FAT 6.8G (SATURATED FAT 2.4G)
PROTEIN 26.5G CARBOHYDRATE 24.0G
CHOLESTEROL 87MG SODIUM 347MG

Choose leeks with crisp, brightly colored leaves and unblemished white portions.

Lesson on Leeks

Leeks belong to the same family as shallots, garlic, and onions but have a milder, more subtle flavor. Although leeks are available year-round, you can find small, tender ones in the spring and fall.

To prepare, cut the root end and then the tough, dark green leaves, leaving the white and light green portions. Slice the leek in half lengthwise, and wash leaves under cold running water.

Creamy Chicken, Leek, and Mushroom Soup

CHUNKY CHICKEN-POTATO SOUP

(pictured on page 64)

Pureeing part of the vegetable mixture helps to thicken the soup.

4 cups canned no-salt-added chicken broth, undiluted
3 cups peeled, cubed baking potato
2 cups chopped onion
1 cup chopped carrot
½ teaspoon salt
⅛ teaspoon ground red pepper
⅛ teaspoon ground black pepper
2 cups chopped cooked chicken breast
¼ cup skim milk
1 (2-ounce) jar diced pimiento, drained
½ cup (2 ounces) shredded reduced-fat sharp Cheddar cheese
½ cup nonfat sour cream
Fresh chives, cut into 1-inch pieces (optional)

Combine first 7 ingredients in a Dutch oven; bring to a boil. Cover, reduce heat, and simmer 35 minutes or until vegetables are tender.

Place half of vegetable mixture in container of an electric blender or food processor; cover and process until smooth. Add pureed mixture, chicken, and milk to mixture in Dutch oven. Cook over medium heat until thoroughly heated, stirring occasionally. Stir in pimiento.

Ladle soup into individual bowls; top evenly with cheese and sour cream. Garnish with chives, if desired. Yield: 8 (1-cup) servings.

PER SERVING: 193 CALORIES (14% FROM FAT)
FAT 3.1G (SATURATED FAT 1.3G)
PROTEIN 19.3G   CARBOHYDRATE 19.7G
CHOLESTEROL 43MG   SODIUM 262MG

GREEK CHICKEN AND RICE SOUP

2 (4-ounce) skinned, boned chicken breast halves
4½ cups canned low-sodium chicken broth, undiluted
½ cup dry white wine
½ cup long-grain rice, uncooked
½ cup wild rice, uncooked
½ cup chopped onion
1 tablespoon minced garlic
2 tablespoons chopped ripe olives
1 teaspoon dried dillweed
½ teaspoon coarsely ground pepper
¼ teaspoon salt
¼ cup frozen egg substitute, thawed
2 tablespoons lemon juice

Combine chicken, broth, and wine in a large Dutch oven. Bring to a boil; cover, reduce heat, and simmer 20 minutes or until chicken is tender. Remove chicken from broth, reserving broth. Let chicken cool slightly. Shred chicken.

Skim fat from broth; add rices, onion, and garlic. Bring to a boil; cover, reduce heat, and simmer 30 minutes. Add shredded chicken, olives, and next 3 ingredients; cover and cook 20 minutes or until wild rice is tender. Combine egg substitute and lemon juice; add to soup, stirring well. Yield: 4 (1½-cup) servings.

PER SERVING: 277 CALORIES (7% FROM FAT)
FAT 2.3G (SATURATED FAT 0.6G)
PROTEIN 20.4G   CARBOHYDRATE 39.8G
CHOLESTEROL 36MG   SODIUM 243MG

Mulligatawny Soup

MULLIGATAWNY SOUP

1 pound skinned, boned chicken thighs
1 tablespoon margarine
1½ cups chopped onion
1 tablespoon curry powder
2 cloves garlic, minced
½ teaspoon salt
⅛ teaspoon pepper
2 (10½-ounce) cans low-salt chicken broth
½ cup all-purpose flour
2 cups 2% low-fat milk
2¾ cups peeled, chopped Golden Delicious
    apple (about 1 pound)
¼ cup chopped fresh parsley

Trim excess fat from chicken; chop chicken, and set aside. Melt margarine in a large saucepan over medium heat. Add onion, curry powder, and garlic; sauté 3 minutes. Add chicken, and sauté 5 minutes. Add salt, pepper, and broth; reduce heat to medium-low, and simmer 10 minutes.

Place flour in a bowl; add milk, stirring with a wire whisk until blended. Add to soup; cook, stirring constantly, 10 minutes or until thickened. Add apple; cook 5 minutes. Remove from heat; stir in parsley. Yield: 8 (1-cup) servings.

PER SERVING: 185 CALORIES (28% FROM FAT)
FAT 5.7G (SATURATED FAT 1.8G)
PROTEIN 15.3G CARBOHYDRATE 18.4G
CHOLESTEROL 52MG SODIUM 270MG

HOT-AND-SOUR SOUP

½ ounce dried shiitake mushrooms
2 cups water
1 (4-ounce) skinned, boned chicken breast half
4½ cups canned no-salt-added chicken broth,
    undiluted
½ cup bamboo shoots, cut into thin strips
½ cup canned shrimp
¼ cup rice vinegar
1 tablespoon sugar
1 tablespoon dry sherry
1 tablespoon low-sodium soy sauce
1½ teaspoons peeled, grated gingerroot
1 teaspoon dark sesame oil
½ teaspoon pepper
¼ teaspoon dry mustard
2½ tablespoons cornstarch
2 tablespoons water
1 egg, beaten
2 tablespoons diagonally sliced green
    onion tops

Combine mushrooms and 2 cups water in a small saucepan. Bring to a boil; remove from heat. Cover and let stand 30 minutes. Drain mushrooms, and cut into thin strips. Set aside.

Place chicken between 2 sheets of heavy-duty plastic wrap; flatten to ¼-inch thickness, using a meat mallet or rolling pin. Cut into thin strips. Combine mushrooms, chicken strips, broth, and next 10 ingredients in a large saucepan. Bring to a boil; cover, reduce heat, and simmer 10 minutes.

Combine cornstarch and 2 tablespoons water; stir well. Add cornstarch mixture to chicken mixture; cook, stirring constantly, 1 minute. Slowly drizzle beaten egg into soup, stirring constantly. (The egg will form lacy strands as it cooks.)

Ladle soup into individual bowls; sprinkle evenly with green onions. Yield: 6 (1-cup) servings.

PER SERVING: 109 CALORIES (18% FROM FAT)
FAT 2.2G (SATURATED FAT 0.5G)
PROTEIN 8.8G   CARBOHYDRATE 9.4G
CHOLESTEROL 66MG   SODIUM 112MG

TORTILLA SOUP

The tortillas absorb some of the soup's liquid and become tender, similar to cooked noodles.

2 (7-inch) flour tortillas
4 (4-ounce) skinned, boned chicken breast
    halves
5 cups canned no-salt-added chicken broth,
    undiluted
1 cup chopped onion
2 teaspoons minced garlic
2 cups frozen corn with red and green
    peppers, thawed
¼ cup chopped green chiles, drained
¼ cup chopped ripe olives
½ teaspoon coarsely ground pepper
¼ teaspoon salt
¼ teaspoon ground cumin
¼ cup chopped fresh cilantro

Cut tortillas into 2- x 1-inch strips. Set aside.

Combine chicken and broth in a large saucepan. Bring to a boil. Cover, reduce heat, and simmer 20 minutes or until chicken is tender. Remove chicken from broth, reserving broth. Let chicken cool slightly. Shred chicken; set aside.

Skim fat from broth; add onion and garlic to broth. Bring to a boil. Cover, reduce heat, and simmer 10 minutes. Add shredded chicken, corn and peppers, and next 5 ingredients. Cook, uncovered, 15 minutes. Add tortilla strips and cilantro; cook 5 minutes. Yield: 8 (1-cup) servings.

PER SERVING: 149 CALORIES (18% FROM FAT)
FAT 2.9G (SATURATED FAT 0.7G)
PROTEIN 15.4G   CARBOHYDRATE 13.8G
CHOLESTEROL 36MG   SODIUM 218MG

THAI CHICKEN SOUP

4 (6-ounce) skinned chicken breast halves
2 quarts water
3 stalks lemon grass, cut into 2-inch pieces
2 small dried red chiles, seeded and minced
2 teaspoons chicken-flavored bouillon granules
8 ounces fresh or frozen, thawed baby corn
1 cup thinly sliced celery
3 tablespoons fresh lime juice
3 tablespoons minced fresh cilantro
3 tablespoons minced green onions
1 small dried red chile, seeded and sliced

Combine first 5 ingredients in a large Dutch oven. Bring to a boil; cover, reduce heat, and simmer 30 minutes or until chicken is tender. Strain broth through a double layer of cheesecloth, reserving broth and chicken. Bone chicken, and cut into ½-inch pieces. Discard bones, and set chicken aside.

Combine chicken broth, corn, and sliced celery in pan; bring to a boil. Add reserved chicken and lime juice; cook over medium heat until soup is thoroughly heated. Ladle soup into individual bowls. Top soup evenly with minced cilantro, minced green onions, and sliced chile. Yield: 8 (1-cup) servings.

PER SERVING: 118 CALORIES (15% FROM FAT)
FAT 2.0G (SATURATED FAT 0.5G)
PROTEIN 17.4G CARBOHYDRATE 8.1G
CHOLESTEROL 44MG SODIUM 287MG

Thai Chicken Soup

SPICY CHICKEN SOUP

*If you make this soup a day ahead of time, the
flavors meld and become more intense.*

1 tablespoon olive oil
1 cup diced sweet onion
2 tablespoons chili powder
1 tablespoon grated orange rind
1 teaspoon dried crushed red pepper
4 cloves garlic, minced
2 cups shredded cooked chicken breast
½ cup fresh orange juice
4 (10½-ounce) cans low-salt chicken broth,
    divided
2 cups sweet red pepper strips
⅓ cup (1-inch) julienne-sliced carrot
⅓ cup diced seeded Anaheim chile
2 tablespoons diced seeded jalapeño pepper
½ teaspoon salt
4 cups coarsely chopped cabbage
4 cups vegetable juice
1 cup wild rice, uncooked
1 tablespoon chili powder
4 plum tomatoes, each cut into eight wedges
3 cups drained canned navy beans
½ cup low-fat sour cream

Heat oil in a large nonstick skillet over medium
heat. Add onion and next 4 ingredients; sauté 4
minutes or until onion is tender. Stir in chicken
and orange juice; bring to a boil. Cook, stirring constantly, 2 minutes or until liquid is almost evaporated. Add 1 can broth; bring to a boil. Stir in sweet
pepper, carrot, Anaheim chile, jalapeño pepper, and
salt. Cook over medium heat 15 minutes or until
vegetables are tender. Set aside.

Combine remaining 3 cans broth, cabbage, and
next 4 ingredients in a large Dutch oven; bring to a
boil. Reduce heat, and simmer, uncovered, 20 minutes. Add chicken mixture and beans; cook, uncovered, 45 additional minutes. Ladle into individual
bowls; top each serving with 1 tablespoon sour
cream. Yield: 8 (1½-cup) servings.

PER SERVING: 383 CALORIES (22% FROM FAT)
FAT 9.3G (SATURATED FAT 2.6G)
PROTEIN 22.4G   CARBOHYDRATE 56.1G
CHOLESTEROL 37MG   SODIUM 881MG

SAUSAGE AND BEAN SOUP

*Tying the onion and herbs in a cheesecloth bag
allows their flavors to seep into the soup and makes
it easy to remove them before serving.*

½ pound dried navy beans
½ pound smoked turkey sausage, sliced
2 cups chopped reduced-fat, low-salt ham
1 cup chopped onion
1 cup chopped celery
½ cup chopped carrot
3½ cups canned no-salt-added beef broth,
    undiluted
1 (14½-ounce) can no-salt-added whole
    tomatoes, undrained and chopped
1 teaspoon dried thyme
½ teaspoon pepper
3 bay leaves
½ small onion
8 black peppercorns
6 whole cloves
2 cloves garlic
1 fresh thyme sprig
1 fresh rosemary sprig
1 fresh oregano sprig

Sort and wash beans; place beans in a large
Dutch oven. Cover with water to depth of 2 inches
above beans. Bring to a boil; cover, remove from
heat, and let stand 1 hour. Drain beans, and return
to Dutch oven. Set aside.

Cook sausage in a large nonstick skillet over
medium heat until browned, stirring frequently.
Drain and pat dry with paper towels. Add sausage,
ham, and next 8 ingredients to beans.

Place onion half and remaining 6 ingredients on a
large piece of cheesecloth; tie ends of cheesecloth
securely. Add to bean mixture. Bring to a boil;
cover, reduce heat, and simmer 1½ hours or until
beans are tender. Remove and discard bay leaves
and cheesecloth bag. Yield: 9 (1-cup) servings.

PER SERVING: 218 CALORIES (30% FROM FAT)
FAT 7.2G (SATURATED FAT 1.9G)
PROTEIN 16.4G   CARBOHYDRATE 21.8G
CHOLESTEROL 46MG   SODIUM 482MG

MINESTRONE WITH TURKEY SAUSAGE

½ pound smoked turkey sausage, cut into
   ¼-inch slices
1 cup diced onion
1 cup diced carrot
¾ cup thinly sliced celery
Vegetable cooking spray
3 cups water
2 cups peeled, diced sweet potato
1 teaspoon dried oregano
½ teaspoon coarsely ground pepper
¼ teaspoon salt
2 (14½-ounce) cans no-salt-added whole
   tomatoes, undrained and coarsely chopped
1 (15-ounce) can Great Northern beans,
   rinsed and drained
8 cups coarsely chopped spinach

Combine first 4 ingredients in a Dutch oven coated with cooking spray; sauté over medium-high heat 7 minutes or until sausage is browned.

Add water and next 6 ingredients to pan. Bring to a boil; cover, reduce heat, and simmer 30 minutes or until vegetables are tender. Stir in spinach; cook 2 additional minutes. Yield: 7 (1½-cup) servings.

PER SERVING: 222 CALORIES (30% FROM FAT)
FAT 7.4G (SATURATED FAT 2.4G)
PROTEIN 12.1G CARBOHYDRATE 29.3G
CHOLESTEROL 0MG SODIUM 525MG

Minestrone with Turkey Sausage

MAKE-AHEAD BRUNSWICK STEW

4 (4-ounce) skinned, boned chicken breast
   halves
2 cups water
2 tablespoons chopped fresh parsley
2 teaspoons minced fresh thyme or ½
   teaspoon dried thyme
½ teaspoon salt
2 bay leaves
1½ cups cubed potato
1 cup sliced celery
1 cup chopped onion
1 (14½-ounce) can no-salt-added whole
   tomatoes, undrained and chopped
1 (10-ounce) package frozen lima beans
1 (10-ounce) package frozen whole-kernel
   corn
2 teaspoons low-sodium Worcestershire sauce
¾ teaspoon pepper
¼ teaspoon hot sauce
¼ teaspoon garlic powder

Combine first 6 ingredients in a large Dutch oven. Bring to a boil; cover, reduce heat, and simmer 20 minutes or until chicken is tender.

Remove chicken from broth; skim fat from broth, reserving broth. Remove and discard bay leaves. Shred chicken, and return to pan. Add potato and next 5 ingredients to pan, stirring well. Add Worcestershire sauce and remaining ingredients. Bring to a boil; cover, reduce heat, and simmer 2 hours, stirring occasionally. Yield: 8 (1-cup) servings.

PER SERVING: 186 CALORIES (9% FROM FAT)
FAT 1.9G (SATURATED FAT 0.5G)
PROTEIN 18.5G CARBOHYDRATE 24.1G
CHOLESTEROL 36MG SODIUM 255MG

Freezing Directions: Place 2 cups stew in each of 4 labeled heavy-duty, zip-top plastic bags. Freeze up to 1 month.

To Serve Two: Thaw 1 (2-cup) bag in refrigerator or microwave oven. Place stew in saucepan, and cook over medium heat until thoroughly heated, stirring occasionally.

Curried Chicken-Vegetable Stew

CURRIED CHICKEN-VEGETABLE STEW

3 (6-ounce) skinned chicken breast halves
3 cups water
¾ cup chopped onion
½ teaspoon dried crushed red pepper
3 cloves garlic, minced
1 (14½-ounce) can no-salt-added whole
    tomatoes, undrained and chopped
2 cups cubed zucchini
2 cups cubed yellow squash
1 cup sliced carrot
1 medium-size sweet red pepper, seeded and
    cut into strips
½ cup no-salt-added tomato sauce
3 tablespoons no-salt-added tomato paste
1 teaspoon ground ginger
½ teaspoon salt
½ teaspoon ground cumin
½ teaspoon ground coriander
¼ teaspoon ground fenugreek

Combine chicken and next 4 ingredients in a
large Dutch oven. Bring mixture to a boil, cover,
reduce heat, and simmer 25 minutes or until
chicken is tender.

Remove chicken from broth; skim fat from broth,
reserving broth. Bone chicken, and cut into bite-
size pieces; discard bones.

Add chicken, chopped tomatoes, and remaining
ingredients to broth in pan; stir well. Bring mixture
to a boil; cover, reduce heat, and simmer 30 minutes
or until vegetables are tender. Yield: 6 (1½-cup)
servings.

PER SERVING: 136 CALORIES (13% FROM FAT)
FAT 1.9G (SATURATED FAT 0.5G)
PROTEIN 16.2G   CARBOHYDRATE 14.6G
CHOLESTEROL 37MG   SODIUM 257MG

CHICKEN 'N' BISCUIT STEW

2 tablespoons reduced-calorie stick margarine
½ cup all-purpose flour
¼ teaspoon salt
¼ teaspoon pepper
½ cup skim milk
1 (10½-ounce) can low-sodium chicken broth
1½ cups cubed cooked chicken breast
⅓ cup chopped onion
1 (8½-ounce) can English peas, drained
1 (8¼-ounce) can sliced carrot, drained
1 (4.5-ounce) can refrigerated buttermilk
   biscuits

Melt margarine in a 9-inch cast-iron skillet over medium-high heat. Stir in flour, salt, and pepper. Gradually add milk and broth, stirring with a wire whisk until blended. Cook, stirring constantly, 4 minutes or until thickened and bubbly. Add chicken, onion, peas, and carrot; cook 1 minute. Remove from heat.

Carefully split biscuits in half horizontally; place over chicken mixture. Bake at 375° for 20 minutes or until biscuits are golden brown. Ladle ¾ cup stew and 2 biscuit halves into each individual bowl. Yield: 5 (¾-cup) servings.

PER SERVING: 268 CALORIES (29% FROM FAT)
FAT 8.7G (SATURATED FAT 1.9G)
PROTEIN 19.9G   CARBOHYDRATE 27.3G
CHOLESTEROL 40MG   SODIUM 645MG

Did You Know?

Curry powder is a blend of up to 20 herbs and spices, including fenugreek, coriander, cumin, pepper, and turmeric. Fenugreek seeds, available either whole or ground, are also used to flavor spice blends and tea. Like other herbs and spices, fenugreek seeds should be stored in a cool, dark place or in the freezer.

TURKEY MEATBALL STEW

1 pound ground raw turkey
½ cup soft breadcrumbs
1 tablespoon chopped fresh parsley
1 teaspoon white wine Worcestershire sauce
½ teaspoon dried marjoram
¼ teaspoon salt
¼ teaspoon dried sage
¼ teaspoon pepper
Vegetable cooking spray
1 teaspoon vegetable oil
2 cups canned low-sodium chicken broth,
   undiluted
1 cup water
2 cups sliced carrot
½ cup chopped onion
½ teaspoon dried thyme
2 cups sliced fresh mushrooms
1 (8-ounce) package frozen Sugar Snap peas,
   thawed

Combine first 8 ingredients in a medium bowl; stir well. Shape into 24 meatballs.

Coat a Dutch oven with cooking spray; add oil. Place over medium heat until hot. Add meatballs, and cook 6 to 8 minutes or until browned, stirring frequently. Drain and pat dry with paper towels. Wipe drippings from pan with a paper towel.

Return meatballs to pan; add broth and next 4 ingredients. Bring to a boil; cover, reduce heat, and simmer 40 minutes or until vegetables are tender. Add mushrooms and peas; stir well. Cover and simmer 10 minutes or until thoroughly heated. Yield: 6 (1-cup) servings.

PER SERVING: 166 CALORIES (19% FROM FAT)
FAT 3.5G (SATURATED FAT 0.9G)
PROTEIN 19.3G   CARBOHYDRATE 13.1G
CHOLESTEROL 49MG   SODIUM 204MG

Easy Turkey-Vegetable Stew

EASY TURKEY-VEGETABLE STEW

2 (10½-ounce) cans low-sodium chicken broth
1 (14½-ounce) can no-salt-added whole
    tomatoes, undrained and chopped
1½ cups sliced carrot
1 cup sliced celery
¾ cup chopped onion
¾ cup water
1 tablespoon chopped fresh basil
2 tablespoons no-salt-added tomato paste
¼ teaspoon salt
¼ teaspoon pepper
¼ teaspoon hot sauce
2 cloves garlic, minced
2½ cups chopped, cooked turkey breast
1 (10-ounce) package frozen English peas,
    thawed
1 (10-ounce) package frozen okra, thawed

Combine chicken broth and next 7 ingredients in a large Dutch oven. Add salt and next 3 ingredients, stirring well. Bring to a boil; cover, reduce heat, and simmer 30 minutes.

Stir turkey, peas, and okra into broth mixture; simmer, uncovered, 10 minutes or until thoroughly heated. Yield: 9 (1-cup) servings.

PER SERVING: 184 CALORIES (5% FROM FAT)
FAT 1.1G (SATURATED FAT 0.3G)
PROTEIN 15.4G   CARBOHYDRATE 26.6G
CHOLESTEROL 31MG   SODIUM 295MG

SAUSAGE AND LENTIL STEW

5 ounces smoked turkey sausage
1½ cups thinly sliced leek (about 1 medium)
2 cloves garlic, minced
¾ cup dried lentils
2 (10½-ounce) cans low-sodium chicken broth
1 teaspoon dried thyme
½ teaspoon sugar
¼ teaspoon hot sauce
2 (14½-ounce) cans no-salt-added stewed
    tomatoes, undrained

Cut sausage into ¼-inch slices; cut each slice in half. Place a large nonstick saucepan over medium-high heat until hot. Add sausage; sauté 3 minutes. Add leek and garlic; cook 3 minutes, stirring occasionally. Add lentils and broth; bring to a boil. Cover, reduce heat, and simmer 30 minutes.

Stir thyme and remaining ingredients into sausage mixture; bring to a boil. Cover, reduce heat, and simmer 15 minutes or until lentils are tender. Yield: 4 (1½-cup) servings.

PER SERVING: 299 CALORIES (19% FROM FAT)
FAT 6.3G (SATURATED FAT 2.1G)
PROTEIN 22.3G   CARBOHYDRATE 41.3G
CHOLESTEROL 29MG   SODIUM 351MG

Sausage and Lentil Stew

Shrimp-Celery Bisque (recipe on page 85)

SEAFOOD SPECIALTIES

*Y*ou know it's smart to eat seafood often, but perhaps you shy away from preparing fish in traditional ways. If so, then try the following soups or stews made with seafood. The cooking time for fish in these dishes is not as sensitive as when cooking it under the broiler or on the grill.

Several delicious bisques open this chapter on pages 85 through 87, followed by soups made with fish or shellfish. A microwave version of Bouillabaisse is featured on page 93. And on page 97, choose from two recipes for a hearty San Francisco classic, Cioppino.

Salmon Bisque

SALMON BISQUE

1 tablespoon vegetable oil
1 cup chopped onion
1 cup chopped celery
4 cups peeled, chopped baking potato
¼ cup finely chopped fresh parsley
1 teaspoon ground white pepper
½ teaspoon salt
2 (14¼-ounce) cans no-salt-added chicken
    broth
¼ cup dry white wine
2 (12-ounce) cans evaporated skimmed milk
1 teaspoon lemon juice
1 (1-pound) salmon fillet, skinned and cut into
    ½-inch pieces
2 tablespoons chopped fresh parsley

Heat oil in a Dutch oven over medium heat. Add onion and celery; sauté 10 minutes or until tender. Add potato and next 4 ingredients. Bring to a boil; cover, reduce heat, and simmer 20 minutes or until potato is tender. Let mixture cool slightly.

Place potato mixture in batches in container of an electric blender or food processor; cover and process until smooth. Return pureed mixture to pan; stir in wine and milk. Cover and cook over medium-low heat 15 minutes, stirring occasionally.

Add lemon juice and salmon; cook 10 minutes or until fish flakes easily when tested with a fork, stirring frequently. Ladle bisque into bowls, and sprinkle evenly with fresh parsley. Yield: 10 (1-cup) servings.

PER SERVING: 186 CALORIES (18% FROM FAT)
FAT 3.8G (SATURATED FAT 0.6G)
PROTEIN 16.4G   CARBOHYDRATE 20.8G
CHOLESTEROL 26MG   SODIUM 287MG

SHRIMP-CELERY BISQUE

(pictured on page 82)

Shrimp and a variety of vegetables fill this hearty bisque with flavor. Use white pepper—it disappears into the bisque, leaving behind its sharpness.

2 cups peeled, diced potato
2 cups chopped celery
3½ cups skim milk, divided
½ cup chopped onion
½ teaspoon ground white pepper
¼ cup all-purpose flour
¾ pound medium-size frozen peeled shrimp,
    thawed and drained
½ cup chopped fresh parsley
2 tablespoons reduced-calorie margarine
½ teaspoon dried thyme
⅛ teaspoon celery seeds
⅛ teaspoon salt
¼ cup dry sherry
Toast points (optional)

Combine potato, celery, 2 cups milk, onion, and pepper in a Dutch oven; cook over medium-high heat, stirring constantly, until mixture comes to a boil. Cover, reduce heat, and simmer 10 to 12 minutes or until potato is tender.

Combine remaining 1½ cups milk and flour in a small bowl; stir well, and add to potato mixture. Add shrimp and next 5 ingredients. Cook over medium-high heat 10 minutes or until thickened and bubbly.

Stir sherry into bisque. Ladle bisque into individual bowls. Serve with toast points, if desired. Yield: 8 (1-cup) servings.

PER SERVING: 165 CALORIES (16% FROM FAT)
FAT 2.9G (SATURATED FAT 0.6G)
PROTEIN 13.9G   CARBOHYDRATE 18.9G
CHOLESTEROL 67MG   SODIUM 214MG

Scallop Bisque

SCALLOP BISQUE

This flavorful bisque can be prepared and cooked in about 30 minutes.

2 (14½-ounce) cans no-salt-added whole
   tomatoes, undrained and coarsely chopped
1 teaspoon sugar
½ teaspoon dried basil
2 tablespoons margarine
¼ cup chopped onion
3 tablespoons all-purpose flour
⅛ teaspoon pepper
1½ cups 1% low-fat milk
1 (8-ounce) bottle clam juice
1 pound bay scallops
2 tablespoons sherry

Combine first 3 ingredients in a large saucepan; cook over medium heat 10 minutes, stirring occasionally. Let cool slightly. Place mixture in container of an electric blender or food processor; cover and process until smooth. Set tomato mixture aside. Wipe pan with a paper towel.

Melt margarine in pan over medium heat. Add onion; sauté 1½ minutes. Add flour and pepper; cook, stirring constantly with a wire whisk, 1 minute. Gradually add milk and clam juice, stirring constantly. Cook, stirring constantly, 5 minutes or until thickened and bubbly. Stir in tomato mixture, scallops, and sherry. Cook 3 minutes or until scallops are opaque. Yield: 7 (1-cup) servings.

PER SERVING: 148 CALORIES (27% FROM FAT)
FAT 4.1G (SATURATED FAT 1.2G)
PROTEIN 14.1G CARBOHYDRATE 13.1G
CHOLESTEROL 23MG SODIUM 254MG

CARIBBEAN FISH SOUP

¾ pound swordfish steaks, cut into 1-inch
   cubes
¼ cup lime juice
1 tablespoon peeled, minced gingerroot
1 jalapeño pepper, seeded and finely diced
2 cloves garlic, minced
Vegetable cooking spray
½ cup sliced green onions
½ cup diced sweet red pepper
2 cups canned vegetable broth, undiluted
½ (8-ounce) bottle clam juice (about ½ cup)
2 cups peeled, seeded, and diced tomato
1 cup peeled, diced papaya
¼ cup minced fresh parsley
¼ teaspoon cracked pepper

Place swordfish in a large glass bowl. Combine lime juice, gingerroot, jalapeño pepper, and garlic. Pour over swordfish; stir gently. Cover and marinate in refrigerator 1 hour, stirring occasionally.

Coat a large saucepan with cooking spray; place over medium-high heat until hot. Add green onions and sweet red pepper; sauté 5 minutes or until tender. Stir in broth and clam juice; bring to a boil. Reduce heat, and simmer, uncovered, 15 minutes. Stir in fish with marinade, tomato, and papaya. Simmer 15 minutes or until fish flakes easily when tested with a fork. Stir in parsley and pepper. Yield: 6 (1-cup) servings.

PER SERVING: 109 CALORIES (25% FROM FAT)
FAT 3.0G (SATURATED FAT 0.7G)
PROTEIN 12.5G CARBOHYDRATE 8.6G
CHOLESTEROL 22MG SODIUM 336MG

Bisque Success

When choosing a Dutch oven for preparing bisques and chowders, select one that allows steady simmering with little risk of scorching. Enameled cast-iron pots and heavy stainless steel or aluminum pans are good choices.

SPICY CRAB SOUP

Vegetable cooking spray
1 cup chopped onion
¾ cup chopped celery
2 cups no-salt-added vegetable juice cocktail
1½ cups peeled, diced potato
1 tablespoon Old Bay seasoning
2 (14½-ounce) cans no-salt-added whole
    tomatoes, undrained and chopped
1 (10½-ounce) can low-sodium chicken broth,
    undiluted
1 pound fresh lump crabmeat, drained
¼ cup chopped fresh parsley

Coat a Dutch oven with cooking spray; place over medium-high heat until hot. Add onion and celery; sauté until tender. Stir in vegetable juice cocktail and next 4 ingredients. Bring to a boil; cover, reduce heat, and simmer 40 to 50 minutes or until potato is tender.

Add crabmeat and parsley to pan; stir well. Cook over low heat 2 minutes or until thoroughly heated. Yield: 10 (1-cup) servings.

PER SERVING: 101 CALORIES (9% FROM FAT)
FAT 1.0G (SATURATED FAT 0.1G)
PROTEIN 10.6G CARBOHYDRATE 12.3G
CHOLESTEROL 43MG SODIUM 323MG

SHE-CRAB SOUP

Butter-flavored vegetable cooking spray
⅔ cup chopped leeks
½ cup chopped celery
2¾ cups evaporated skimmed milk
2½ cups peeled, diced red potato
1 cup canned no-salt-added chicken broth,
    undiluted
¼ teaspoon salt
⅛ teaspoon ground white pepper
2 tablespoons dry sherry
½ pound fresh lump crabmeat, drained

Coat a large saucepan with cooking spray; place over medium-high heat until hot. Add leeks and celery; sauté until tender. Stir in milk and next 4

ingredients. Bring to a boil; reduce heat, and simmer 20 minutes or until potato is tender. Let cool slightly.

Transfer mixture in batches to container of an electric blender or food processor; cover and process until smooth. Return mixture to saucepan; stir in sherry and crabmeat. Cook over medium heat 5 minutes or until heated. Yield: 8 (1-cup) servings.

PER SERVING: 137 CALORIES (7% FROM FAT)
FAT 1.1G (SATURATED FAT 0.2G)
PROTEIN 13.5G CARBOHYDRATE 17.8G
CHOLESTEROL 32MG SODIUM 281MG

CRABMEAT-CORN SOUP

Vegetable cooking spray
1⅓ cups chopped purple onion
1⅓ cups chopped celery
¾ cup chopped green pepper
3 cloves garlic, minced
4 cups water
1 tablespoon Worcestershire sauce
½ teaspoon salt
½ teaspoon dried thyme
¼ teaspoon pepper
2 (10½-ounce) cans low-salt chicken broth
1 (16-ounce) package frozen shoepeg white
    corn
1 (10-ounce) can diced tomatoes and green
    chiles, undrained
1 (6-ounce) can tomato paste
1 cup sliced green onions
1 pound fresh lump crabmeat, shell pieces
    removed and drained

Coat a Dutch oven with cooking spray; place over medium heat until hot. Add onion and next 3 ingredients, and sauté 5 minutes. Add water and next 8 ingredients; bring to a boil. Reduce heat, and simmer, uncovered, 1 hour. Stir in green onions and crabmeat; cook over medium heat 15 minutes. Yield: 12 (1-cup) servings.

PER SERVING: 113 CALORIES (13% FROM FAT)
FAT 1.6G (SATURATED FAT 0.3G)
PROTEIN 10.4G CARBOHYDRATE 15.6G
CHOLESTEROL 38MG SODIUM 356MG

Oyster-Artichoke Soup

OYSTER-ARTICHOKE SOUP

1 (16-ounce) container standard oysters,
   undrained
1 teaspoon margarine
½ cup chopped green onions
3 (8-ounce) bottles clam juice
1 tablespoon chopped fresh parsley
½ teaspoon dried thyme
¼ teaspoon ground red pepper
¼ cup plus 2 tablespoons all-purpose flour
2 cups 2% low-fat milk
1 (14-ounce) can quartered artichoke hearts,
   drained
Sliced green onions (optional)
Freshly ground black pepper (optional)

Drain oysters, reserving ¼ cup juice; set both aside. Melt margarine in a large saucepan over medium-high heat. Add ½ cup chopped green onions; sauté 3 minutes. Add reserved oyster juice, clam juice, and next 3 ingredients; bring to a boil. Reduce heat, and simmer, uncovered, 10 minutes.

Place flour in a bowl. Gradually add milk, stirring with a wire whisk until blended; gradually add to soup, stirring well. Cook over medium heat, stirring constantly, 6 minutes or until thickened. Stir in oysters and artichokes, and cook 3 minutes or until edges of oysters curl. Pour into bowls; if desired, garnish with sliced green onions and black pepper. Yield: 7 (1-cup) servings.

PER SERVING: 127 CALORIES (26% FROM FAT)
FAT 3.7G (SATURATED FAT 1.4G)
PROTEIN 8.9G   CARBOHYDRATE 14.8G
CHOLESTEROL 41MG   SODIUM 443MG

BRAZILIAN SHELLFISH SOUP

1 pound small clams in shells, scrubbed (about 20 clams)

1 pound small mussels, scrubbed and debearded (about 30 mussels)

1 tablespoon cornmeal

½ pound unpeeled medium-size fresh shrimp

2 cups water

1 tablespoon vegetable oil

2 cups chopped onion

1 cup chopped sweet red pepper

1 cup chopped sweet yellow pepper

1 tablespoon minced seeded jalapeño pepper

4 cloves garlic, minced

4 cups peeled, chopped tomato

2 tablespoons peeled, grated gingerroot

2 teaspoons grated orange rind

3 (8-ounce) bottles clam juice

1 (6-ounce) can tomato paste

2 tablespoons minced green onions

2 tablespoons chopped fresh parsley

2 tablespoons chopped fresh cilantro

½ teaspoon salt

½ teaspoon pepper

1 (12-ounce) can evaporated skim milk

3 tablespoons shredded sweetened coconut, toasted

Cilantro sprigs (optional)

Brazilian Shellfish Soup

Discard open, cracked, or heavy clams and mussels. Set aside remaining mussels. Place clams in a bowl; cover with cold water. Sprinkle with cornmeal; let stand 30 minutes. Drain and rinse clams, discarding cornmeal; set aside.

Peel and devein shrimp; set aside.

Bring 2 cups water to a boil in a Dutch oven. Add clams and mussels; cover and cook 6 minutes or until shells open. Discard any unopened shells. Remove clams and mussels from pan; set aside. Discard cooking liquid. Heat oil in pan over medium heat. Add 2 cups onion and next 4 ingredients; sauté 8 minutes. Add tomato and next 4 ingredients; cook 15 minutes, stirring occasionally. Add shrimp; cook 3 minutes or until shrimp turn pink. Remove from heat; stir in clams, mussels, green onions, and next 5 ingredients. Ladle soup into individual bowls; sprinkle each with 1½ teaspoons coconut. Garnish with cilantro sprigs, if desired. Yield: 6 (2-cup) servings.

PER SERVING: 221 CALORIES (22% FROM FAT)
FAT 5.3G (SATURATED FAT 1.7G)
PROTEIN 16.5G CARBOHYDRATE 29.9G
CHOLESTEROL 51MG SODIUM 627MG

MUSSEL AND MUSHROOM SOUP

Vegetable cooking spray
1½ teaspoons olive oil
2 cloves garlic, minced
2 cups sliced fresh mushrooms
1 cup peeled, seeded, and chopped tomato
1⅓ cups dry white wine
½ teaspoon dried thyme
Dash of ground red pepper
1 (2-inch) strip orange rind
3 pounds fresh mussels, scrubbed and debearded
2 tablespoons chopped fresh parsley
8 (¼-inch) diagonally cut slices French bread, toasted

Coat a large Dutch oven with cooking spray; add oil. Place over medium heat until hot. Add garlic, and sauté 1 minute. Add mushrooms and next 5 ingredients; bring to a boil.

Discard any open, cracked, or heavy mussels. Spread remaining mussels, hinged side down, over wine mixture. Cover and cook over medium-high heat 6 minutes or until mussels open. Discard orange rind and any unopened mussel shells.

Spoon 1 cup wine mixture into each shallow bowl; top each with one-fourth of mussels and 1½ teaspoons parsley. Serve each with 2 slices toast. Yield: 4 servings.

PER SERVING: 223 CALORIES (21% FROM FAT)
FAT 5.3G (SATURATED FAT 0.9G)
PROTEIN 16.2G CARBOHYDRATE 27.5G
CHOLESTEROL 29MG SODIUM 488MG

TEX-MEX SEAFOOD SOUP

4½ cups water, divided
½ pound unpeeled small fresh shrimp
½ pound fresh bay scallops
5 cups peeled, chopped tomato, divided
2 cups peeled, chopped cucumber, divided
1 cup chopped sweet red pepper, divided
3 tablespoons lime juice
1 tablespoon minced jalapeño pepper
½ teaspoon ground cumin
1 clove garlic, thinly sliced
1 (6-ounce) can spicy hot vegetable juice cocktail

Bring 4 cups water to a boil. Add shrimp; cook 3 minutes or until shrimp turn pink. Drain; rinse with cold water. Peel and devein shrimp; cover and chill.

Bring remaining ½ cup water to a boil; add scallops. Cover, reduce heat, and simmer 2 minutes. Drain well; rinse with cold water. Cover and chill.

Combine 4 cups tomato, 1 cup cucumber, ½ cup sweet red pepper, and next 5 ingredients in container of an electric blender or food processor; cover and process until smooth. Pour into a bowl; stir in remaining 1 cup tomato, 1 cup cucumber, and ½ cup sweet red pepper. Cover and chill. Stir in shrimp and scallops. Yield: 5 (1½-cup) servings.

PER SERVING: 141 CALORIES (11% FROM FAT)
FAT 1.8G (SATURATED FAT 0.3G)
PROTEIN 17.0G CARBOHYDRATE 15.9G
CHOLESTEROL 67MG SODIUM 269MG

SHRIMP WONTON SOUP

Stirring the broth mixture while adding the
wontons keeps them from sticking together.

1 pound unpeeled medium-size fresh shrimp
¼ cup sliced green onions
1 tablespoon water
2 teaspoons cornstarch
2 teaspoons lemon juice
1½ teaspoons dark sesame oil
1 teaspoon peeled, grated gingerroot
¼ teaspoon sugar
1 (8-ounce) can sliced water chestnuts,
    drained
36 wonton wrappers
1 egg white, lightly beaten
3 cups water
2 (14½-ounce) cans Oriental broth
¼ cup (½-inch) diagonally sliced green onions

Peel and devein shrimp. Place shrimp, green
onions, and next 7 ingredients in a food processor;
pulse 6 times or until coarsely chopped.

Working with 1 wonton wrapper at a time (cover
remaining wrappers with a damp towel to keep
them from drying out), spoon about 1 tablespoon
shrimp mixture into center of wrapper. Moisten
edges of wrapper with egg white, and bring 2 oppo-
site corners together. Pinch edges together to seal,
forming a triangle. Moisten 2 bottom points of triangle with egg white, and bring points together,
overlapping about ½ inch; pinch together to seal.
Repeat procedure with remaining wonton wrappers, shrimp mixture, and egg white.

Combine 3 cups water and broth in a large Dutch
oven; bring to a boil. Stir broth mixture while adding wontons; cook 1½ minutes or until wontons are
tender. Ladle 1 cup soup into each individual bowl;
add 6 wontons to each, and sprinkle each with 2
teaspoons diagonally sliced green onions. Yield:
6 servings.

Note: Oriental broth can typically be found next
to the canned chicken broth in the supermarket.

PER SERVING: 241 CALORIES (11% FROM FAT)
FAT 2.9G (SATURATED FAT 0.5G)
PROTEIN 17.8G CARBOHYDRATE 34.8G
CHOLESTEROL 91MG SODIUM 1083MG

SHRIMP-TORTELLINI SOUP

½ pound unpeeled medium-size fresh shrimp
2 quarts water
½ (9-ounce) package refrigerated cheese
    tortellini, uncooked
1½ cups broccoli flowerets
2 teaspoons olive oil
¾ cup sliced crimini mushrooms
2 tablespoons chopped purple onion
½ teaspoon ground ginger
¼ teaspoon salt
1 (14¼-ounce) can fat-free chicken broth
Purple onion slices, separated into rings
    (optional)

Peel and devein shrimp; set aside.

Bring water to a boil in a large saucepan. Add
tortellini; cook 4 minutes. Add broccoli, and cook 5
additional minutes or until tortellini is tender.
Drain in a colander; set aside.

Heat oil in pan over medium-high heat. Add
shrimp, mushrooms, and chopped onion; sauté 3
minutes or until shrimp turn pink. Add ginger, salt,
and broth; bring to a boil. Add tortellini mixture,
and cook until thoroughly heated. Ladle soup into
individual bowls, and garnish with onion rings, if
desired. Yield: 4 (1-cup) servings.

Note: Because this recipe uses only half the package of tortellini, freeze the remaining half in an airtight container.

PER SERVING: 215 CALORIES (24% FROM FAT)
FAT 5.8G (SATURATED FAT 1.5G)
PROTEIN 21.3G CARBOHYDRATE 20.1G
CHOLESTEROL 100MG SODIUM 440MG

Bouillabaisse

BOUILLABAISSE

4 medium-size red potatoes (about
  1½ pounds)
1 pound unpeeled medium-size fresh shrimp
2 (8-ounce) bottles clam juice
1 (14½-ounce) can no-salt-added whole
  tomatoes, drained
1½ cups thinly sliced onion
¼ cup chopped fresh parsley
½ cup dry white wine
1½ tablespoons tomato paste
1 tablespoon olive oil
½ teaspoon dried thyme
¼ teaspoon salt
¼ teaspoon threads of saffron
¼ teaspoon pepper
⅛ teaspoon fennel seeds
2 cloves garlic, minced
2 slices lemon
1 bay leaf
¾ pound cod or other lean white fish fillets,
  cut into 1-inch pieces

Pierce potatoes with a fork. Arrange potatoes in a circle on a paper towel in microwave oven. Microwave at HIGH 10 minutes, rearranging potatoes after 5 minutes. Wrap potatoes in a towel, and let stand 5 minutes. Peel and cube potatoes; set aside.

Peel and devein shrimp; set aside.

Combine clam juice and next 14 ingredients in a 3-quart casserole; stir well. Cover and microwave at HIGH 10 minutes, stirring after 5 minutes. Stir in potato, shrimp, and fish. Cover and microwave at HIGH 3 minutes or until fish flakes easily when tested with a fork. Discard bay leaf. Yield: 5 (1½-cup) servings.

Note: Turmeric may be substituted for saffron, if desired.

PER SERVING: 257 CALORIES (15% FROM FAT)
FAT 4.4G (SATURATED FAT 0.7G)
PROTEIN 26.9G CARBOHYDRATE 27.6G
CHOLESTEROL 111MG SODIUM 450MG

PORTUGUESE FISH STEW

Olive oil flavored-vegetable cooking spray
1 teaspoon olive oil
1½ cups chopped onion
⅓ cup sliced carrot
2 cloves garlic, minced
2¼ cups peeled, seeded, and chopped tomato
2 cups peeled, cubed potato
2 cups thinly sliced leeks
1 cup chopped green pepper
¾ cup water
¼ cup dry white wine
2 teaspoons grated lemon rind
½ teaspoon dried thyme
¼ teaspoon salt
¼ teaspoon pepper
1 pound unpeeled medium-size fresh shrimp
1 pound flounder fillets, cut into 1-inch pieces
Chopped fresh parsley (optional)

Coat a Dutch oven with cooking spray; add oil. Place over medium-high heat until hot. Add onion, carrot, and garlic; sauté until vegetables are crisp-tender. Add tomato and next 9 ingredients, stirring well. Bring mixture to a boil over medium heat; cover, reduce heat, and simmer 20 minutes.

Peel and devein shrimp. Add shrimp and flounder to vegetable mixture, stirring well. Cover and simmer 10 to 15 minutes or until fish flakes easily when tested with a fork and shrimp turn pink. Ladle stew into individual bowls; garnish with parsley, if desired. Yield: 8 (1-cup) servings.

PER SERVING: 166 CALORIES (13% FROM FAT)
FAT 2.4G (SATURATED FAT 0.4G)
PROTEIN 21.2G   CARBOHYDRATE 14.8G
CHOLESTEROL 92MG   SODIUM 194MG

RED SNAPPER STEW

Vegetable cooking spray
2 cups chopped onion
1 cup chopped celery
½ cup chopped green pepper
1 clove garlic, minced
1½ cups water
1 cup dry white wine
1 teaspoon chicken-flavored bouillon granules
¼ teaspoon salt
¼ teaspoon ground red pepper
1 large potato (½ pound), peeled and cut into
    1-inch cubes
1 (14½-ounce) can whole tomatoes, undrained
    and chopped
1 bay leaf
1½ pounds red snapper fillets, skinned and cut
    into 1-inch pieces
Chopped fresh parsley (optional)

Coat a Dutch oven with cooking spray; place over medium heat until hot. Add onion, celery, green pepper, and garlic to pan; sauté until vegetables are tender. Stir in water and next 7 ingredients; bring to a boil. Cover, reduce heat, and simmer 20 minutes.

Add fish to stew; cover and simmer 10 minutes or until fish flakes easily when tested with a fork. Remove and discard bay leaf. Ladle into serving bowls, and sprinkle with parsley, if desired. Yield: 8 (1-cup) servings.

PER SERVING: 167 CALORIES (10% FROM FAT)
FAT 1.8G (SATURATED FAT 0.4G)
PROTEIN 24.3G   CARBOHYDRATE 12.8G
CHOLESTEROL 40MG   SODIUM 341MG

Red Snapper Stew

Cioppino

CIOPPINO

10 littleneck clams
1 tablespoon cornmeal
½ pound unpeeled large fresh shrimp
Vegetable cooking spray
1 teaspoon olive oil
1½ cups chopped onion
½ cup chopped green pepper
2½ tablespoons chopped fresh parsley
1 large clove garlic, minced
2 (8-ounce) cans no-salt-added tomato sauce
1⅔ cups canned tomato puree
1¼ cups canned no-salt-added chicken broth, undiluted
½ cup dry red wine
½ teaspoon dried thyme
½ teaspoon dried oregano
¼ teaspoon pepper
¼ teaspoon hot sauce
1 bay leaf
½ pound red snapper fillets, cut into 2-inch pieces
¼ pound fresh sea scallops

Scrub clam shells thoroughly, discarding any that are open or cracked. Place clams in a large bowl; cover with cold water. Sprinkle with cornmeal; let stand 30 minutes. Drain and rinse clams, discarding cornmeal; set clams aside.

Peel and devein shrimp; set aside.

Coat a large Dutch oven with cooking spray; add oil. Place over medium-high heat until hot. Add onion, green pepper, parsley, and garlic; sauté until tender. Add tomato sauce and next 8 ingredients; bring to a boil. Cover, reduce heat, and simmer 20 minutes, stirring occasionally.

Add clams, shrimp, red snapper, and scallops to pan; bring to a boil. Reduce heat, and simmer 8 to 10 minutes or until clam shells open and fish flakes easily when tested with a fork. Remove and discard bay leaf and any unopened clams. Yield: 6 (1½-cup) servings.

PER SERVING: 189 CALORIES (13% FROM FAT)
FAT 2.8G (SATURATED FAT 0.5G)
PROTEIN 22.9G   CARBOHYDRATE 18.5G
CHOLESTEROL 77MG   SODIUM 441MG

GRILLED SEAFOOD CIOPPINO

¾ pound unpeeled medium-size fresh shrimp
1 tablespoon plus 1 teaspoon olive oil, divided
1 (8-ounce) sourdough baguette, cut crosswise into 12 slices
1½ cups chopped onion
3 cloves garlic, minced
½ cup dry white wine
1 teaspoon dried basil
1 teaspoon dried thyme
½ teaspoon hot sauce
¼ teaspoon salt
¼ teaspoon threads of saffron
2 (14½-ounce) cans stewed tomatoes
2 cups canned low-sodium chicken broth, undiluted
12 small mussels, scrubbed and debearded
¾ pound skinned sea bass, halibut, or snapper fillet, cut into 1-inch pieces
Vegetable cooking spray

Peel and devein shrimp; set aside. Brush 2 teaspoons oil over 1 side of bread slices; set aside.

Heat remaining 2 teaspoons oil in a large saucepan over medium heat. Add onion and garlic; sauté 5 minutes or until tender. Add wine and next 7 ingredients, and bring to a boil. Reduce heat, and simmer 20 minutes, stirring occasionally.

Discard open, cracked, or heavy mussels. Add remaining mussels to saucepan; cover and simmer 5 minutes or until shells open (discard any unopened shells). Remove from heat. Set aside; keep warm.

Thread shrimp and fish alternately onto each of 6 (9-inch) skewers. Coat grill rack with cooking spray; place on grill over medium-hot coals (350° to 400°). Place kabobs and bread slices on rack, and grill 6 minutes or until seafood is done and bread is toasted, turning both occasionally.

Ladle 1 cup soup into each of 6 bowls; top with grilled seafood, and serve each with 2 slices toasted bread. Yield: 6 servings.

PER SERVING: 325 CALORIES (20% FROM FAT)
FAT 7.3G (SATURATED FAT 1.7G)
PROTEIN 30.9G   CARBOHYDRATE 33.6G
CHOLESTEROL 108MG   SODIUM 843MG

California Seafood Stew

CALIFORNIA SEAFOOD STEW

½ pound unpeeled medium-size fresh shrimp
Vegetable cooking spray
½ cup chopped onion
½ cup chopped sweet red pepper
1 clove garlic, minced
1 (14½-ounce) can no-salt-added whole
   tomatoes, undrained and chopped
1 (8-ounce) can no-salt-added tomato sauce
¼ cup dry red wine
¼ cup chopped fresh oregano
2 tablespoons chopped fresh parsley
1 teaspoon low-sodium Worcestershire sauce
¼ teaspoon dried crushed red pepper
½ pound bay scallops
1 (10-ounce) can whole baby clams, drained

Peel and devein shrimp; set aside.

Coat a Dutch oven with cooking spray; place over medium-high heat until hot. Add chopped onion, sweet red pepper, and minced garlic; sauté until vegetables are tender.

Add tomatoes, tomato sauce, and wine, stirring well to combine. Add oregano and next 3 ingredients; stir well. Bring vegetable mixture to a boil over medium heat; cover, reduce heat, and simmer 20 minutes. Add shrimp, scallops, and clams to vegetable mixture; bring to a boil. Reduce heat, and simmer 7 to 8 minutes or until scallops are opaque and shrimp turn pink. Yield: 6 (1-cup) servings.

PER SERVING: 146 CALORIES (10% FROM FAT)
FAT 1.6G (SATURATED FAT 0.2G)
PROTEIN 20.9G   CARBOHYDRATE 11.6G
CHOLESTEROL 77MG   SODIUM 160MG

SHELLFISH ENCHILADOS

20 fresh mussels, scrubbed and debearded
1 pound unpeeled medium-size fresh shrimp
Vegetable cooking spray
1 cup coarsely chopped onion
2 cloves garlic, minced
1 cup diced sweet red pepper
1 cup diced green pepper
2 cups peeled, seeded, and chopped plum
    tomato
1 tablespoon minced jalapeño pepper
⅛ teaspoon threads of saffron
⅛ teaspoon salt
6 whole allspice, crushed
1 bay leaf
1 cup dark beer

Discard open, cracked, or heavy mussels (they're filled with sand). Set aside remaining mussels.

Peel and devein shrimp; set aside.

Coat a large Dutch oven with cooking spray, and place over medium-low heat until hot. Add onion and garlic, and sauté 2 minutes; add red and green peppers, and sauté 2 minutes. Stir in tomato and remaining 6 ingredients; bring to a boil. Reduce heat, and simmer, uncovered, 5 minutes.

Add shrimp; spread mussels, hinged side down, over shrimp and vegetable mixture. Cover and cook over medium heat 5 minutes or until shrimp turn pink and mussels open. Discard bay leaf and any unopened mussels. Ladle 1 cup soup into each individual bowl; top each with 4 mussels. Yield: 5 servings.

PER SERVING: 141 CALORIES (15% FROM FAT)
FAT 2.3G (SATURATED FAT 0.4G)
PROTEIN 17.8G   CARBOHYDRATE 12.7G
CHOLESTEROL 109MG   SODIUM 230MG

Shellfish Enchilados

Tortellini, Bean, and Basil Soup (recipe on page 103)

VEGETABLE MEDLEY

*M*other was right, after all! Vegetables really are good for you. What's so great about them? They supply fiber, carbohydrates, vitamins, and minerals—nutrients that are essential to healthy living.

One of the easiest ways to increase your family's intake of vegetables is with soup. You might prefer one of the hearty bean soups on pages 102 through 105 or a simple cream soup made with asparagus or broccoli on page 106. You'll find soups made with mushrooms, potatoes, spinach, and squash. There's even a creamy tomato soup on page 116 whose flavor far surpasses the canned version.

Closing out the chapter is a recipe for Garden Vegetable Soup (page 121). It's old-fashioned in flavor but up-to-date in its unusually low fat content.

Cuban Black Bean Soup

CUBAN BLACK BEAN SOUP

3 (15-ounce) cans no-salt-added black beans,
   undrained
2 (14¼-ounce) cans no-salt-added beef broth
2 cups water
1½ cups chopped onion
¾ cup chopped green pepper
2 teaspoons minced garlic
1 (14½-ounce) can no-salt-added whole
   tomatoes, undrained and chopped
1 (4½-ounce) can chopped green chiles
¼ pound lean cooked ham, diced
½ cup red wine vinegar
1 teaspoon dried oregano
1 teaspoon dried thyme
1 teaspoon ground cumin
½ teaspoon coarsely ground pepper
Fresh cilantro sprigs (optional)

Combine beans, broth, water, onion, green pepper, and garlic in a large Dutch oven; bring mixture to a boil. Cover, reduce heat, and simmer 20 minutes, stirring frequently.

Add tomatoes and next 7 ingredients to bean mixture. Cook, uncovered, over low heat 30 minutes, stirring occasionally. Ladle into individual bowls; garnish with cilantro, if desired. Yield: 10 (1½-cup) servings.

PER SERVING: 220 CALORIES (6% FROM FAT)
FAT 1.5G (SATURATED FAT 0.4G)
PROTEIN 14.8G   CARBOHYDRATE 37.4G
CHOLESTEROL 6MG   SODIUM 161MG

BEAN AND BARLEY SOUP

1 tablespoon olive oil
1 cup chopped onion
1 cup chopped carrot
½ cup chopped celery
2 cloves garlic, minced
½ cup pearl barley, uncooked
¼ pound smoked turkey sausage, cut into
    ½-inch cubes
2 cups frozen baby lima beans
1¾ cups water
⅛ teaspoon pepper
2 (14¼-ounce) cans fat-free chicken broth
1 (14½-ounce) can diced tomatoes, undrained
½ teaspoon hot sauce

Heat oil in a Dutch oven over medium-high heat. Add onion and next 3 ingredients; sauté 5 minutes. Add barley and sausage; sauté 4 minutes. Add beans and next 4 ingredients; bring to a boil. Reduce heat, and simmer, uncovered, 45 minutes. Stir in hot sauce. Yield: 6 (1½-cup) servings.

PER SERVING: 228 CALORIES (26% FROM FAT)
FAT 6.7G (SATURATED FAT 1.6G)
PROTEIN 13.4G   CARBOHYDRATE 29.5G
CHOLESTEROL 16MG   SODIUM 423MG

BEANS AND GREENS SOUP

Vegetable cooking spray
1½ cups chopped onion
1½ cups chopped carrot
1 clove garlic, minced
4 cups water
1 (15-ounce) can pinto beans, rinsed and
    drained
¼ cup chopped fresh parsley
1 teaspoon chicken-flavored bouillon granules
½ teaspoon dried thyme
¼ teaspoon ground red pepper
1 bay leaf
3 cups coarsely chopped kale
¾ cup diced lean smoked turkey ham

Coat a large Dutch oven with cooking spray; place over medium-high heat until hot. Add onion, carrot, and garlic; sauté until vegetables are crisp-tender.

Add water and next 6 ingredients to pan; stir well. Bring to a boil; cover, reduce heat, and simmer 10 minutes. Add kale and ham. Cover and cook 5 additional minutes or until thoroughly heated. Remove and discard bay leaf. Yield: 4 (1½-cup) servings.

PER SERVING: 206 CALORIES (12% FROM FAT)
FAT 2.8G (SATURATED FAT 0.8G)
PROTEIN 14.2G   CARBOHYDRATE 33.4G
CHOLESTEROL 0MG   SODIUM 907MG

TORTELLINI, BEAN, AND BASIL SOUP

(pictured on page 100)

4 cups canned low-sodium chicken broth,
    undiluted
1 (9-ounce) package refrigerated cheese-filled
    tortellini, uncooked
1 (15-ounce) can cannellini beans, drained
1 cup chopped tomato
½ cup shredded fresh basil
2 tablespoons balsamic vinegar
¼ teaspoon salt
⅓ cup freshly grated Parmesan cheese
1½ teaspoons freshly ground pepper

Bring broth to a boil in a large Dutch oven. Add tortellini, and cook 6 minutes or until tender. Stir in beans and tomato. Reduce heat, and simmer 5 minutes or until thoroughly heated. Remove from heat; stir in basil, vinegar, and salt.

Ladle soup into individual bowls; sprinkle evenly with cheese and pepper. Yield: 7 (1-cup) servings.

PER SERVING: 185 CALORIES (20% FROM FAT)
FAT 4.1G (SATURATED FAT 1.9G)
PROTEIN 11.3G   CARBOHYDRATE 25.9G
CHOLESTEROL 18MG   SODIUM 409MG

TUSCAN VEGETABLE SOUP

1 whole head garlic
3 cups canned vegetable broth, undiluted
1 tablespoon olive oil
1 cup chopped purple onion
1 cup diced sweet red pepper
1 cup diced fennel bulb
1 cup diced zucchini
1 teaspoon dried oregano
3½ cups cooked penne (about 8 ounces
     uncooked tubular pasta), cooked without
     salt or fat
1 cup diced tomato
1 (15-ounce) can cannellini beans or other
     white beans, drained
1 sprig thyme
1 sprig rosemary
1 cup coarsely chopped escarole
¼ teaspoon freshly ground pepper

Remove white papery skin from garlic head (do not peel or separate cloves). Wrap garlic head in aluminum foil, and bake at 350° for 1 hour; let cool 10 minutes. Separate cloves, and squeeze to extract pulp; discard skins.

Combine garlic pulp and broth in a medium saucepan; bring to a boil. Reduce heat, and simmer 5 minutes. Set aside.

Heat olive oil in a Dutch oven over medium-high heat. Add onion and next 4 ingredients; sauté 2 minutes. Add broth mixture, pasta, and next 4 ingredients; bring to a boil. Reduce heat; simmer 5 minutes or until vegetables are tender. Remove from heat; stir in escarole and pepper. Discard thyme and rosemary. Yield: 6 (1⅓-cup) servings.

PER SERVING: 231 CALORIES (16% FROM FAT)
FAT 4.0G (SATURATED FAT 0.4G)
PROTEIN 8.6G CARBOHYDRATE 41.1G
CHOLESTEROL 0MG SODIUM 493MG

Tuscan Vegetable Soup

ITALIAN MINESTRONE

½ pound dried red kidney beans
1 tablespoon olive oil
1 cup thinly sliced leeks
1 cup julienne-sliced carrot
½ cup sliced celery
2 tablespoons minced fresh parsley
1 tablespoon minced fresh garlic
1 tablespoon dried basil
½ teaspoon dried thyme
½ teaspoon dried oregano
¼ teaspoon salt
⅛ teaspoon ground red pepper
5 cups water
2 (10½-ounce) cans low-sodium chicken broth
2 (14½-ounce) cans no-salt-added whole
    tomatoes, undrained and coarsely chopped
1 cup elbow macaroni, uncooked
2 cups coarsely shredded cabbage
1½ cups thinly sliced zucchini
½ (10-ounce) package frozen chopped
    spinach, thawed
¼ cup freshly grated Parmesan cheese

Sort and wash beans; place in a Dutch oven. Cover with water to depth of 2 inches above beans; let soak overnight.

Drain beans well; set aside. Add olive oil to pan; place over medium-high heat until hot. Add leeks and next 4 ingredients; sauté until tender. Stir in basil and next 4 ingredients; sauté 1 minute. Stir in beans, 5 cups water, and chicken broth; bring to a boil. Cover, reduce heat, and simmer 1 hour or until beans are tender, stirring occasionally.

Stir in tomatoes and next 4 ingredients. Bring to a boil; reduce heat, and simmer 15 minutes. Ladle into individual bowls; top each serving with 1 teaspoon cheese. Yield: 12 (1-cup) servings.

PER SERVING: 172 CALORIES (14% FROM FAT)
FAT 2.6G (SATURATED FAT 0.7G)
PROTEIN 9.2G CARBOHYDRATE 29.6G
CHOLESTEROL 2MG SODIUM 142MG

HEARTY LENTIL SOUP

1 teaspoon olive oil
½ pound dried lentils
1 cup coarsely chopped onion
1 teaspoon chili powder
2 cups peeled, cubed potato
⅓ cup diced carrot
½ cup chopped 96% fat-free, low-sodium ham
7 cups water
1 (14¼-ounce) can no-salt-added chicken
    broth
1 teaspoon dry mustard
1 teaspoon peeled, grated gingerroot
½ teaspoon ground coriander
½ teaspoon dried thyme
4 bay leaves
2 cloves garlic, crushed
¼ teaspoon salt
¼ teaspoon freshly ground pepper
¼ cup plus 3 tablespoons plain nonfat yogurt

Heat oil in a large Dutch oven over medium heat until hot. Add lentils, onion, and chili powder; sauté 2 minutes or until lentils are golden. Add potato and next 10 ingredients. Bring to a boil; reduce heat, and simmer, uncovered, 2 hours, stirring occasionally. Stir in salt and pepper. Remove and discard bay leaves. Ladle soup into individual bowls. Top each serving with 1 tablespoon yogurt. Yield: 7 (1-cup) servings.

PER SERVING: 182 CALORIES (8% FROM FAT)
FAT 1.6G (SATURATED FAT 0.2G)
PROTEIN 13.5G CARBOHYDRATE 29.5G
CHOLESTEROL 6MG SODIUM 196MG

FYI

What if you want to prepare Italian Minestrone but have no leeks in the refrigerator? Since leeks are related to onions, substitute an equal amount of mild, sweet onion for the leeks. For tips on selecting and preparing leeks, turn to page 70.

ASPARAGUS SOUP

The potato helps give this soup its thick, creamy consistency without adding fat.

1¾ pounds fresh asparagus
1 cup peeled, cubed potato
Vegetable cooking spray
1 tablespoon reduced-calorie margarine
¼ cup finely chopped onion
¼ cup finely chopped celery
¼ cup chopped fresh parsley
1 tablespoon chopped fresh basil
1 tablespoon all-purpose flour
1 (14¼-ounce) can no-salt-added chicken
   broth
1 cup 1% low-fat milk
2 teaspoons lemon juice
¼ teaspoon salt
Lemon zest (optional)

Snap off tough ends of asparagus. Remove scales from stalks with a knife or vegetable peeler, if desired. Cut asparagus into 2-inch pieces. Place asparagus pieces and cubed potato in a large saucepan. Add water to cover. Bring to a boil. Cover, reduce heat, and simmer 10 minutes or until potato is tender; drain well.

Coat a large saucepan with cooking spray, and add margarine. Place over medium-high heat until margarine melts. Add onion and celery; sauté until vegetables are tender. Reduce heat to low. Add parsley, basil, and flour; cook, stirring constantly, 1 minute. Gradually add chicken broth; cook over medium heat, stirring constantly, 5 minutes. Stir in asparagus mixture; let cool slightly.

Pour vegetable mixture in batches into container of an electric blender or food processor; cover and process until smooth. Return mixture to saucepan. Add milk, lemon juice, and salt; cook until thoroughly heated, stirring frequently.

To serve, ladle soup into individual bowls. Garnish with lemon zest, if desired. Yield: 6 (1-cup) servings.

PER SERVING: 87 CALORIES (21% FROM FAT)
FAT 2.0G (SATURATED FAT 0.5G)
PROTEIN 4.6G CARBOHYDRATE 13.8G
CHOLESTEROL 2MG SODIUM 146MG

FRESH BROCCOLI SOUP

2 pounds fresh broccoli
1 cup chopped onion
¾ cup diced carrot
½ cup chopped celery
1 cup water
2 tablespoons reduced-calorie margarine
2½ tablespoons all-purpose flour
2½ cups 1% low-fat milk
1½ cups canned low-sodium chicken broth,
   undiluted
3 ounces light process American cheese, cubed
½ teaspoon pepper
½ teaspoon low-sodium Worcestershire sauce
¼ teaspoon salt

Trim off large leaves of broccoli, and remove tough ends of lower stalks. Wash broccoli thoroughly, and coarsely chop.

Place broccoli in a large Dutch oven; add water to depth of 1 inch. Bring to a boil; cover, reduce heat, and simmer 15 minutes or until broccoli is tender, stirring occasionally. Drain and set aside.

Combine onion, carrot, celery, and 1 cup water in a small saucepan. Bring to a boil; reduce heat, and simmer 20 minutes or until vegetables are tender. Remove from heat, and let cool slightly. Transfer vegetables and water to container of an electric blender or food processor; cover and process until smooth.

Melt margarine in pan over medium heat; add flour. Cook, stirring constantly with a wire whisk, 1 minute. Gradually add milk, stirring constantly, and cook until thickened and bubbly. Add broccoli, pureed vegetables, chicken broth, and remaining ingredients; stir well. Cook over low heat, stirring constantly, until cheese melts. Yield: 9 (1-cup) servings.

PER SERVING: 129 CALORIES (27% FROM FAT)
FAT 3.9G (SATURATED FAT 1.4G)
PROTEIN 9.1G CARBOHYDRATE 16.7G
CHOLESTEROL 8MG SODIUM 321MG

CREAM OF CELERY SOUP

Vegetable cooking spray
1 teaspoon vegetable oil
1 (8-ounce) package sliced fresh mushrooms
1 cup chopped onion
2¾ cups thinly sliced celery
2 cups water
¼ cup chopped fresh parsley
1½ teaspoons chicken-flavored bouillon
    granules
½ teaspoon dried sage
⅛ teaspoon ground white pepper
3½ tablespoons all-purpose flour
2 cups skim milk, divided
2 tablespoons sliced almonds, toasted

Coat a Dutch oven with cooking spray; add oil. Place over medium-high heat until hot. Add mushrooms and onion; sauté until vegetables are tender. Stir in celery and next 5 ingredients. Bring to a boil; cover, reduce heat, and simmer 15 minutes, stirring occasionally.

Combine flour and ¼ cup milk; stir until smooth. Add flour mixture and remaining 1¾ cups milk to mushroom mixture; stir well. Cook over medium heat, stirring constantly, until slightly thickened and bubbly. Ladle soup into individual bowls; sprinkle evenly with toasted almonds. Yield: 6 (1-cup) servings.

PER SERVING: 94 CALORIES (28% FROM FAT)
FAT 2.9G (SATURATED FAT 0.4G)
PROTEIN 5.3G   CARBOHYDRATE 13.4G
CHOLESTEROL 2MG   SODIUM 291MG

EGG DROP SOUP

½ cup boiling water
¼ ounce dried wood ear mushrooms
1½ cups canned no-salt-added chicken broth,
    undiluted
1 tablespoon dry sherry
1 tablespoon reduced-sodium soy sauce
⅛ teaspoon pepper
Dash of salt
1 egg, lightly beaten
2 tablespoons chopped green onions

Combine water and mushrooms; cover and let stand 20 minutes. Drain, reserving ½ cup mushroom liquid. Discard mushroom stems. Thinly slice mushroom caps.

Combine sliced mushroom caps, reserved mushroom liquid, chicken broth, and next 4 ingredients in a medium saucepan; bring to a boil. Slowly drizzle egg into soup, stirring constantly with a fork. Reduce heat to low, and cook, stirring constantly, 1 minute. Ladle into individual bowls, and sprinkle with green onions. Yield: 4 (1-cup) servings.

PER SERVING: 41 CALORIES (29% FROM FAT)
FAT 1.3G (SATURATED FAT 0.4G)
PROTEIN 2.0G   CARBOHYDRATE 2.5G
CHOLESTEROL 55MG   SODIUM 117MG

Egg Drop Soup

SPRINGTIME GREEN PEA SOUP

1¼ pounds fresh English peas
1 teaspoon olive oil
2 cups chopped leeks
1 cup chopped onion
1½ cups peeled, cubed baking potato
½ cup chopped parsnips
½ cup water
½ teaspoon dried thyme
1 (14¼-ounce) can no-salt-added chicken broth
3 tablespoons dry white wine
¼ teaspoon salt
⅛ teaspoon ground white pepper
¼ cup plus 1 tablespoon plain low-fat yogurt

Shell and wash peas; set aside.

Heat oil in a large saucepan over medium-high heat. Add leeks and onion; sauté 5 minutes. Add potato and next 4 ingredients; bring to a boil. Cover, reduce heat, and simmer 15 minutes. Add peas; cover and simmer 20 additional minutes or until peas are tender. Let mixture cool slightly.

Spoon mixture in batches into container of an electric blender or food processor; cover and process until mixture is smooth. Return puree to pan; add wine, salt, and pepper. Cook over low heat until thoroughly heated. Ladle soup into individual bowls, and top each with 1 tablespoon yogurt. Yield: 5 (1-cup) servings.

Note: You may want to purchase fresh English peas already shelled. For this recipe, you will need 1¼ cups shelled English peas.

PER SERVING: 144 CALORIES (10% FROM FAT)
FAT 1.6G (SATURATED FAT 0.3G)
PROTEIN 5.4G CARBOHYDRATE 27.5G
CHOLESTEROL 1MG SODIUM 144MG

CREAM OF MUSHROOM SOUP

Skim milk and nonfat sour cream combine for a rich and creamy but low-fat soup base.

Vegetable cooking spray
¾ pound sliced fresh mushrooms
¼ cup sliced green onions
2 tablespoons dry sherry
2 tablespoons reduced-calorie stick margarine
3 tablespoons all-purpose flour
2½ cups skim milk
1¼ teaspoons chicken-flavored bouillon granules
¼ teaspoon freshly ground pepper
⅔ cup nonfat sour cream
Green onion strips (optional)

Coat a large saucepan with cooking spray; place over medium-high heat until hot. Add mushrooms, ¼ cup green onions, and sherry; sauté until vegetables are tender. Set aside.

Melt margarine in a medium-size heavy saucepan over medium heat; add flour, stirring until smooth. Cook, stirring constantly, 1 minute. Gradually add milk to flour mixture; cook over medium heat, stirring constantly, 10 minutes or until mixture is thickened and bubbly.

Stir in mushroom mixture, bouillon granules, and pepper. Cook until thoroughly heated. Remove from heat, and stir in sour cream. Ladle soup into individual bowls. Garnish with green onion strips, if desired. Yield: 4 (1-cup) servings.

PER SERVING: 161 CALORIES (27% FROM FAT)
FAT 4.8G (SATURATED FAT 0.8G)
PROTEIN 10.5G CARBOHYDRATE 19.4G
CHOLESTEROL 3MG SODIUM 423MG

Cream of Mushroom Soup

French Onion Soup

6 (½-inch) slices French bread baguette
Vegetable cooking spray
1 tablespoon margarine
6 cups thinly sliced onion (about 3 large)
½ teaspoon sugar
⅛ teaspoon pepper
3 tablespoons all-purpose flour
4 (14¼-ounce) cans no-salt-added beef broth
1 (10-ounce) can beef consommé, undiluted
½ cup dry white wine
1 tablespoon Worcestershire sauce
6 thin slices (1½ ounces) Gruyère cheese

Place baguette slices on a baking sheet, and bake at 375° for 8 minutes or until lightly browned; set aside.

Coat a Dutch oven with cooking spray; add margarine, and place over medium-low heat until margarine melts. Add onion, and sauté 5 minutes.

Sprinkle onion with sugar and pepper. Reduce heat to low; cook 20 minutes or until onion is golden, stirring often. Sprinkle onion with flour; cook, stirring constantly, 2 minutes. Add broth, consommé, and wine. Bring to a boil; reduce heat, and simmer, partially covered, 30 minutes. Remove from heat, and stir in Worcestershire sauce.

Ladle 1½ cups soup into each of 6 ovenproof soup bowls; top each serving with 1 slice bread and 1 slice cheese. Place soup bowls on a large baking sheet, and broil 5½ inches from heat (with electric oven door partially opened) 1 minute or until cheese melts. Yield: 6 (1½-cup) servings.

Note: Substitute ½ cup canned no-salt-added beef broth, undiluted, for ½ cup dry white wine, if desired.

PER SERVING: 204 CALORIES (23% FROM FAT)
FAT 5.1G (SATURATED FAT 1.9G)
PROTEIN 8.0G   CARBOHYDRATE 28.7G
CHOLESTEROL 8MG   SODIUM 522MG

Onion and Roasted Garlic Bisque

1 large whole head garlic
1½ tablespoons olive oil, divided
9 cups thinly sliced Vidalia or other sweet onion (about 4 large)
2½ cups sliced leeks (about 2 medium)
1 teaspoon salt, divided
1 teaspoon dried thyme
2 tablespoons all-purpose flour
⅓ cup dry white wine
3 (10½-ounce) cans low-sodium chicken broth
2 cups 2% low-fat milk
¼ cup plus 2 tablespoons nonfat sour cream
Fresh chives (optional)
Toasted caraway seeds (optional)

Remove white papery skin from garlic head (do not peel or separate cloves). Rub 1½ teaspoons oil over garlic head; wrap in foil. Bake at 350° for 1 hour; let cool 10 minutes. Separate cloves; squeeze to extract garlic pulp. Discard skins, and set garlic pulp aside.

Heat remaining 1 tablespoon oil in a large Dutch oven over medium heat. Add onion and leeks; cook 30 minutes, stirring often. Add ½ teaspoon salt and thyme. Cook 30 additional minutes or until onion is golden, stirring occasionally. Stir in flour. Add wine and broth; bring to a boil. Reduce heat, and simmer 30 minutes.

Add garlic pulp, remaining ½ teaspoon salt, and milk to onion mixture; simmer 8 minutes or until thoroughly heated. Let mixture cool slightly.

Place half of onion mixture in container of an electric blender or food processor; cover and process until smooth. Pour pureed mixture into a bowl; repeat procedure with remaining onion mixture. Ladle soup into individual bowls, and garnish each with 1 tablespoon sour cream and, if desired, chives and caraway seeds. Yield: 6 (1-cup) servings.

PER SERVING: 249 CALORIES (24% FROM FAT)
FAT 6.6G (SATURATED FAT 1.8G)
PROTEIN 9.8G   CARBOHYDRATE 40.1G
CHOLESTEROL 7MG   SODIUM 510MG

ROASTED GARLIC-POTATO SOUP

Thickened by mashed potatoes, this rich soup gets its hearty, smoky flavor from the addition of bacon and garlic.

5 whole heads garlic
2 slices bacon, diced
1 cup diced onion
1 cup diced carrot
2 cloves garlic, minced
6 cups peeled, diced baking potato (about 2 pounds)
4 cups canned low-sodium chicken broth, undiluted
½ teaspoon salt
¼ teaspoon pepper
1 bay leaf
1 cup 2% low-fat milk
¼ cup chopped fresh parsley
Additional chopped fresh parsley (optional)

Remove white papery skin from each garlic head (do not peel or separate cloves). Wrap each head separately in aluminum foil. Bake at 350° for 1 hour; let cool 10 minutes. Separate cloves, and squeeze to extract ¼ cup garlic pulp. Discard skins, and set pulp aside.

Cook bacon in a large saucepan over medium-high heat until crisp. Add onion, carrot, and minced garlic; sauté 5 minutes. Add potato, broth, salt, pepper, and bay leaf; bring to a boil. Cover, reduce heat, and simmer 20 minutes or until potato is tender; remove bay leaf.

Combine garlic pulp and 2 cups potato mixture in container of an electric blender or food processor; cover and process until smooth. Return puree to potato mixture in pan; stir in milk, and cook over low heat until thoroughly heated. Remove from heat, and stir in ¼ cup chopped parsley. Sprinkle with additional parsley, if desired. Yield: 7 (1-cup) servings.

PER SERVING: 199 CALORIES (14% FROM FAT)
FAT 3.0G (SATURATED FAT 1.1G)
PROTEIN 7.8G CARBOHYDRATE 38.0G
CHOLESTEROL 5MG SODIUM 300MG

Roasted Garlic-Potato Soup

SWEET POTATO SOUP

2 cups peeled, cubed sweet potato
1½ cups thinly sliced leeks (about 1 medium)
1¼ cups canned fat-free chicken broth, undiluted and divided
⅔ cup evaporated skim milk
½ teaspoon salt
1½ teaspoons Dijon mustard
Dash of ground white pepper
Dash of ground nutmeg

Combine sweet potato, leeks, and ¼ cup broth in a 1½-quart casserole; stir well. Cover and microwave at HIGH 10 minutes, stirring after 5 minutes; let cool slightly.

Place sweet potato mixture in container of an electric blender or food processor; cover and process until smooth. Add remaining 1 cup broth, milk, and remaining 4 ingredients; cover and process 30 seconds or until blended. Return to saucepan, and cook until thoroughly heated. Ladle into individual bowls. Yield: 3 (1-cup) servings.

PER SERVING: 181 CALORIES (3% FROM FAT)
FAT 0.7G (SATURATED FAT 0.1G)
PROTEIN 6.7G CARBOHYDRATE 36.3G
CHOLESTEROL 3MG SODIUM 555MG

Five-Spice Red Pepper Soup

FIVE-SPICE RED PEPPER SOUP

2 large sweet red peppers (about 1¼ pounds)
1 teaspoon olive oil
1 cup chopped onion
1 teaspoon Chinese five-spice powder
2 cloves garlic, minced
½ cup tomato paste
¼ cup water
¼ teaspoon salt
⅛ teaspoon pepper
2 (10½-ounce) cans low-sodium chicken broth
¼ cup plus 1 tablespoon nonfat sour cream

Cut red peppers in half lengthwise; discard seeds and membranes. Place peppers, skin side up, on a baking sheet; flatten with palm of hand. Broil peppers 3 inches from heat (with electric oven door partially opened) 10 minutes or until blackened and charred. Place peppers in ice water, and chill 5 minutes. Drain peppers; peel and discard skins. Set peppers aside.

Heat oil in a large saucepan over medium heat. Add onion, five-spice powder, and garlic; sauté 5 minutes. Add peppers, tomato paste, and next 4 ingredients; stir well. Bring to a boil; cover, reduce heat, and simmer 10 minutes. Let mixture cool slightly.

Spoon mixture in batches into container of an electric blender or food processor; cover and process until smooth. Ladle into individual bowls; top each with 1 tablespoon sour cream. Yield: 5 (1-cup) servings.

PER SERVING: 79 CALORIES (24% FROM FAT)
FAT 2.1G (SATURATED FAT 0.2G)
PROTEIN 3.9G CARBOHYDRATE 12.4G
CHOLESTEROL 0MG SODIUM 186MG

CREAMY SPINACH SOUP

3 (1-ounce) slices white bread
½ pound fresh spinach
2 teaspoons margarine
1 cup chopped onion
1 clove garlic, minced
1 cup water
2 teaspoons beef-flavored bouillon granules
2 medium baking potatoes, peeled and cubed
1 bay leaf
3½ cups skim milk
¼ cup instant nonfat dry milk powder
4 ounces Neufchâtel cheese, cubed
¼ teaspoon pepper

Trim crusts from bread slices; reserve crusts for another use. Cut bread into ¾-inch cubes; arrange in a single layer in a 15- x 10- x 1-inch jellyroll pan. Bake at 350° for 12 minutes or until golden, stirring twice. Set croutons aside.

Remove stems from spinach; wash leaves, and pat dry with paper towels. Set spinach aside.

Melt margarine in a large Dutch oven over medium-high heat. Add onion and garlic; sauté until tender. Add spinach, water, and next 3 ingredients to onion mixture. Bring to a boil; cover, reduce heat, and simmer 15 to 20 minutes or until potato is tender, stirring occasionally. Remove and discard bay leaf. Let mixture cool slightly.

Pour spinach mixture into container of an electric blender or food processor; cover and process until smooth, stopping once to scrape down sides. Return puree to Dutch oven.

Combine milk and milk powder; stir well. Add to spinach mixture; stir well. Stir in cheese and pepper. Cook over medium heat until cheese melts and mixture is thoroughly heated, stirring frequently. Ladle soup into individual bowls. Top evenly with croutons. Yield: 7 (1-cup) servings.

PER SERVING: 198 CALORIES (26% FROM FAT)
FAT 5.8G (SATURATED FAT 3.0G)
PROTEIN 10.4G CARBOHYDRATE 26.7G
CHOLESTEROL 16MG SODIUM 502MG

Apple-Butternut Soup

APPLE-BUTTERNUT SOUP

Vegetable cooking spray
1 tablespoon reduced-calorie margarine
1 cup chopped onion
1 clove garlic, minced
1 tablespoon all-purpose flour
1 (10½-ounce) can low-sodium chicken broth
3 cups peeled, seeded, and cubed butternut
  squash
1⅓ cups peeled, cored, and coarsely chopped
  cooking apple
¼ teaspoon dried thyme
⅛ teaspoon salt
½ cup 1% low-fat milk
Toasted squash seeds (optional)
Fresh thyme sprigs (optional)
Nonfat sour cream (optional)

Coat a Dutch oven with cooking spray; add margarine. Place over medium heat until margarine melts. Add onion and garlic; sauté 5 minutes or until tender. Add flour, stirring until smooth. Stir in chicken broth and next 4 ingredients; bring to a boil. Cover, reduce heat, and simmer 45 minutes or until squash is tender. Let mixture cool slightly.

Position knife blade in food processor bowl; add squash mixture. Process 1 minute or until smooth, scraping sides of processor bowl once.

Return mixture to pan; add milk. Cook over medium heat until thoroughly heated, stirring occasionally (do not boil). Ladle soup into individual bowls. If desired, garnish with squash seeds, thyme sprigs, and sour cream. Yield: 4 (1-cup) servings.

PER SERVING: 129 CALORIES (22% FROM FAT)
FAT 3.1G (SATURATED FAT 0.7G)
PROTEIN 3.4G CARBOHYDRATE 24.8G
CHOLESTEROL 1MG SODIUM 146MG

SUMMER SQUASH SOUP

Vegetable cooking spray
2 teaspoons reduced-calorie margarine
1 cup chopped onion
2 tablespoons chopped fresh parsley
1½ teaspoons minced fresh basil
1¾ pounds yellow squash, cut into ¼-inch
  slices
1 medium zucchini, cut into ¼-inch slices
1 cup canned no-salt-added chicken broth,
  undiluted
½ teaspoon salt
⅛ teaspoon ground white pepper
1 cup skim milk
Chopped fresh chives (optional)

Coat a Dutch oven with cooking spray; add margarine. Place over medium-high heat until margarine melts. Add onion, parsley, and basil; sauté until onion is tender. Add yellow squash and next 4 ingredients; cover and cook over medium heat 15 to 20 minutes or until squash is tender, stirring occasionally. Add milk; cook, stirring constantly, until mixture is thoroughly heated.

Transfer mixture in batches to container of an electric blender or food processor; cover and process until smooth. Return puree to pan. Cook over medium heat just until thoroughly heated (do not boil).

Ladle soup into individual bowls. Garnish with chopped fresh chives, if desired. Yield: 5 (1-cup) servings.

PER SERVING: 77 CALORIES (23% FROM FAT)
FAT 2.0G (SATURATED FAT 0.4G)
PROTEIN 4.5G CARBOHYDRATE 11.9G
CHOLESTEROL 1MG SODIUM 307MG

Winter Squash and White Bean Soup

WINTER SQUASH AND WHITE BEAN SOUP

A bowlful of this soup counts as two of the five recommended daily servings of fruits and vegetables.

1 tablespoon vegetable oil
1 cup finely chopped onion
¾ teaspoon ground cinnamon
½ teaspoon ground cumin
1 clove garlic, minced
3 cups peeled, cubed butternut squash (about 1½ pounds)
⅛ teaspoon pepper
2 (10½-ounce) cans low-sodium chicken broth
1 (14½-ounce) can Mexican-style stewed tomatoes, undrained
1 (14½-ounce) can no-salt-added whole tomatoes, undrained and chopped
1 (16-ounce) can cannellini beans, drained

Heat oil in a large Dutch oven over medium heat. Add onion and next 3 ingredients; sauté 5 minutes or until onion is tender. Add squash and next 4 ingredients; bring to a boil. Cover, reduce heat, and simmer 30 minutes or until squash is tender. Let mixture cool slightly.

Place 2 cups squash mixture in container of an electric blender or food processor; cover and process until smooth. Return squash puree to pan. Stir in beans; cook over medium heat 5 minutes or until thoroughly heated. Yield: 6 (1½-cup) servings.

PER SERVING: 168 CALORIES (19% FROM FAT)
FAT 3.5G (SATURATED FAT 0.7G)
PROTEIN 7.2G   CARBOHYDRATE 29.9G
CHOLESTEROL 0MG   SODIUM 341MG

FRESH TOMATO SOUP

1 teaspoon margarine
2 tablespoons minced shallots
3 cups peeled, seeded, and diced tomato (about 2 pounds)
¾ cup 2% low-fat milk
½ cup canned low-sodium chicken broth, undiluted
½ teaspoon salt
Dash of ground white pepper
Chopped fresh oregano leaves (optional)

Melt margarine in a large saucepan over medium-low heat; add shallots. Cover and cook 5 minutes or until tender. Add tomato; cover and cook 15 minutes. Let cool slightly.

Place tomato mixture in container of an electric blender or food processor; cover and process until smooth. Add milk and next 3 ingredients; cover and process 5 seconds. Return tomato mixture to pan, and cook over medium heat 8 minutes or until heated. Garnish with fresh oregano, if desired. Yield: 4 (1-cup) servings.

PER SERVING: 87 CALORIES (28% FROM FAT)
FAT 2.7G (SATURATED FAT 0.8G)
PROTEIN 3.9G   CARBOHYDRATE 13.9G
CHOLESTEROL 4MG   SODIUM 358MG

Fresh Tomato Soup

Tomato-Egg Flower Soup

TOMATO-EGG FLOWER SOUP

1 (14¼-ounce) can no-salt-added chicken broth
1 (14½-ounce) can no-salt-added whole tomatoes, undrained and chopped
1 teaspoon reduced-sodium soy sauce
1 egg white
¼ teaspoon sesame oil
¼ teaspoon salt
¼ teaspoon freshly ground pepper
1 green onion, diagonally sliced
Tomato rose (optional)

Combine broth and tomatoes in a large saucepan; bring to a boil. Remove from heat; add soy sauce.

Combine egg white and oil. Stir hot broth mixture vigorously with a wire whisk while gradually adding egg white mixture. Add salt and pepper.

To serve, ladle soup into individual bowls; top with sliced green onion, and garnish with tomato rose, if desired. Yield: 4 (1-cup) servings.

PER SERVING: 37 CALORIES (7% FROM FAT)
FAT 0.3G (SATURATED FAT 0.0G)
PROTEIN 1.9G CARBOHYDRATE 5.7G
CHOLESTEROL 0MG SODIUM 208MG

Tomato Roses

To make the tomato rose garnish shown at left, cut a thin slice from bottom of tomato, using a sharp paring knife; discard. Beginning at top, peel a continuous paper-thin strip (about ¾ inch wide) from entire tomato.

Beginning with first portion cut, shape the strip like a rose. With flesh side inward, coil the strip tightly at first to form the center of rose, gradually letting it become looser to form the outer petals.

Use the green portion of a green onion to make leaves for the rose.

ROASTED TOMATO-SHALLOT SOUP

To shave Parmesan cheese into thin slivers, pull a vegetable peeler across the top of a wedge of fresh Parmesan.

2 pounds plum tomatoes, cut in half
2 shallots, peeled and cut in half
2 large cloves garlic, cut in half
1 jalapeño pepper, cut in half and seeded
Vegetable cooking spray
½ (9-ounce) package refrigerated light cheese-filled ravioli, uncooked
2 teaspoons chopped fresh oregano
⅛ teaspoon dried marjoram
1 cup canned low-sodium chicken broth, undiluted
1 tablespoon lemon juice
1 teaspoon sugar
1 teaspoon balsamic vinegar
1 ounce shaved fresh Parmesan cheese
Fresh oregano sprigs (optional)

Combine first 4 ingredients in a shallow baking pan coated with cooking spray. Bake at 350° for 40 minutes.

Cook ravioli according to package directions, omitting salt and fat; drain and set aside.

Place roasted vegetables in container of an electric blender or food processor; add chopped oregano and marjoram. Cover and process until smooth.

Pour tomato mixture into a large saucepan. Stir in cooked ravioli, broth, lemon juice, sugar, and vinegar. Cook over medium heat until thoroughly heated, stirring frequently. Ladle soup into individual bowls; top evenly with cheese. Garnish with oregano sprigs, if desired. Yield: 4 (1-cup) servings.

PER SERVING: 194 CALORIES (24% FROM FAT)
FAT 5.1G (SATURATED FAT 2.1G)
PROTEIN 10.6G CARBOHYDRATE 29.3G
CHOLESTEROL 27MG SODIUM 283MG

VEGETABLE-BARLEY SOUP

(pictured on page 2)

Vegetable cooking spray
1 cup chopped onion
½ cup chopped celery
2 tablespoons chopped fresh parsley
1 clove garlic, minced
7 cups water
1 cup thinly sliced carrot
½ cup barley, uncooked
1 tablespoon beef-flavored bouillon granules
¼ teaspoon pepper
¼ teaspoon dried oregano
¼ teaspoon dried basil
¼ teaspoon dried thyme
¼ teaspoon curry powder
1 (28-ounce) can whole tomatoes, undrained
    and chopped
1 bay leaf
1 cup thinly sliced leeks
1 cup shredded cabbage
½ cup peeled, diced turnips

Coat a large Dutch oven with cooking spray; place over medium heat until hot. Add onion, celery, parsley, and garlic; sauté until vegetables are tender.

Add water and next 10 ingredients; stir well, and bring to a boil. Cover, reduce heat, and simmer 20 minutes. Stir in leeks, cabbage, and turnips; cover and simmer 15 minutes. Remove and discard bay leaf. Yield: 12 (1-cup) servings.

PER SERVING: 64 CALORIES (6% FROM FAT)
FAT 0.4G (SATURATED FAT 0.1G)
PROTEIN 2.3G   CARBOHYDRATE 14.0G
CHOLESTEROL 0MG   SODIUM 374MG

VEGETABLE-CHEESE SOUP

Vegetable cooking spray
1⅓ cups finely chopped onion
1 cup thinly sliced carrot
½ cup thinly sliced green onions
½ cup thinly sliced celery
2 (10½-ounce) cans low-sodium chicken broth
2 cups peeled, diced red potato
¼ cup long-grain rice, uncooked
4 ounces reduced-fat loaf process cheese
    spread, cubed
2 cups 1% low-fat milk
2 tablespoons diced pimiento
¼ teaspoon salt
¼ teaspoon black pepper
⅛ teaspoon garlic powder
⅛ teaspoon ground red pepper

Coat a Dutch oven with cooking spray; place over medium-high heat until hot. Add onion, carrot, green onions, and celery; sauté until tender. Add chicken broth, potato, and rice; bring to a boil. Reduce heat, and simmer 20 minutes or until vegetables are tender. Remove from heat, and let cool 10 minutes.

Transfer vegetable mixture in batches to container of an electric blender or food processor; cover and process until smooth. Return mixture to pan. Stir in cheese and remaining ingredients. Cook over medium heat, stirring constantly, until cheese melts and mixture is smooth. Yield: 7 (1-cup) servings.

PER SERVING: 158 CALORIES (22% FROM FAT)
FAT 3.9G (SATURATED FAT 1.6G)
PROTEIN 8.0G   CARBOHYDRATE 23.0G
CHOLESTEROL 11MG   SODIUM 420MG

GARDEN VEGETABLE SOUP

2 quarts canned no-salt-added beef broth,
    undiluted
3 cups chopped tomato
2 cups diced potato
2 cups chopped cabbage
1 cup frozen whole-kernel corn
½ cup chopped carrot
½ cup chopped onion
½ cup chopped zucchini
½ cup chopped fresh green beans
1 teaspoon salt
1 teaspoon dried Italian seasoning
½ teaspoon pepper
½ teaspoon hot sauce
1 (6-ounce) can no-salt-added tomato paste
1 bay leaf

Place broth in a large saucepan; bring to a boil. Add tomato and remaining ingredients. Reduce heat, and simmer, uncovered, 1 hour, stirring occasionally. Remove and discard bay leaf. Yield: 8 (1½-cup) servings.

PER SERVING: 122 CALORIES (3% FROM FAT)
FAT 0.4G (SATURATED FAT 0.1G)
PROTEIN 4.1G   CARBOHYDRATE 25.1G
CHOLESTEROL 0MG   SODIUM 330MG

Freezing Directions: Place 3 cups soup in each of 4 labeled airtight containers. Freeze up to 1 month.

To Serve Two: Thaw 1 (3-cup) container in refrigerator or microwave oven. Place soup in a medium saucepan. Cover and cook over medium heat until thoroughly heated, stirring occasionally.

Garden Vegetable Soup

Louisiana Turkey-Seafood Gumbo (recipe on page 138)

CHILIES, CHOWDERS & GUMBOS

*A*bout as many versions of chili exist as there are cooks who make it. Made with or without beans, with or without meat, and with varying degrees of heat, the combinations of chili ingredients are almost endless. Starting on page 125 are several chili recipes that have at least one thing in common—they're low in fat.

Equally satisfying, especially in cold weather, are chowders and gumbos. The chowder recipes on pages 130 through 136 have the typical richness of chowder without the fat. The gumbos featured are also low in fat, thanks to the technique given on page 137 for making roux.

Finally, you'll find a stew-like ragoût and Kentucky Burgoo on pages 138 and 140. Both are loaded with meat and vegetables and make for filling meals on frosty days.

Chipotle-Black Bean Chili

CHIPOTLE-BLACK BEAN CHILI

Chipotle chiles frequently come packaged in adobo sauce (a Mexican-type red sauce) and can be very hot. They're usually found in the Mexican section of your supermarket. Substitute ¼ teaspoon ground pepper for the chipotle, if desired.

1 teaspoon olive oil
1 cup finely chopped onion
6 cloves garlic, minced
2 tablespoons chili powder
1 teaspoon minced drained canned chipotle
     chile in adobo sauce
¼ teaspoon pepper
⅛ teaspoon salt
2 (15-ounce) cans black beans, drained
2 (14½-ounce) cans no-salt-added whole
     tomatoes, undrained and chopped
1 (4.5-ounce) can chopped green chiles,
     drained
Cilantro sprigs (optional)

Heat oil in a large saucepan over medium-high heat. Add onion and garlic; sauté 3 minutes or until tender. Add chili powder and next 6 ingredients; bring to a boil. Reduce heat; simmer 15 minutes. Ladle chili into individual bowls; garnish with cilantro sprigs, if desired. Yield: 4 (1½-cup) servings.

PER SERVING: 248 CALORIES (10% FROM FAT)
FAT 2.7G (SATURATED FAT 0.5G)
PROTEIN 13.8G CARBOHYDRATE 46.6G
CHOLESTEROL 0MG   SODIUM 613MG

Quick Chili

Homemade chili in less than 40 minutes? Using canned beans shortens preparation and cooking times. If you prefer to use dried beans, follow the instructions for soaking beans on page 105 in the recipe for Italian Minestrone.

JAMAICAN CHILI

(pictured on cover)

Vegetable cooking spray
1 teaspoon olive oil
1½ cups chopped onion
2 cloves garlic, crushed
2½ cups chopped sweet yellow pepper
1 tablespoon ground cumin
1 tablespoon hot Hungarian paprika
1 tablespoon chili powder
2 teaspoons sugar
½ teaspoon salt
¼ teaspoon ground cloves
1 cup water
2 tablespoons no-salt-added tomato paste
2 (14½-ounce) cans no-salt-added stewed
     tomatoes, undrained
1 (15-ounce) can kidney beans, drained
1 (15-ounce) can cannellini beans, drained
1 (15-ounce) can black beans, drained
2 tablespoons balsamic vinegar
¼ cup plus 2 tablespoons minced fresh cilantro

Coat a Dutch oven with cooking spray; add oil. Place over medium-high heat until hot. Add onion and garlic; sauté until onion is tender. Add yellow pepper; sauté until pepper is tender. Add cumin and next 5 ingredients; sauté 1 minute.

Stir in water and next 5 ingredients; bring to a boil. Cover, reduce heat, and simmer 20 minutes.

Remove from heat; stir in vinegar. Ladle chili into individual bowls. Top each serving with 1 tablespoon cilantro. Yield: 6 (1⅔-cup) servings.

PER SERVING: 266 CALORIES (8% FROM FAT)
FAT 2.5G (SATURATED FAT 0.3G)
PROTEIN 14.3G CARBOHYDRATE 50.0G
CHOLESTEROL 0MG   SODIUM 554MG

Vegetable Chili

VEGETABLE CHILI

2 cups chopped onion
1 cup chopped green pepper
1 (14¼-ounce) can no-salt-added beef broth
¼ cup sliced ripe olives
2 tablespoons chili powder
1 teaspoon ground coriander
1 teaspoon dried oregano
1 teaspoon pepper
1 (2-pound) eggplant, cubed
2 (15-ounce) cans kidney beans, drained
2 (10¾-ounce) cans low-sodium tomato soup
½ cup (2 ounces) finely shredded reduced-fat
   sharp Cheddar cheese

Combine first 3 ingredients in a Dutch oven. Bring broth mixture to a boil; cover, reduce heat, and simmer 15 minutes.

Add olives and next 7 ingredients; cover and cook 50 additional minutes or until vegetables are tender, stirring occasionally. Ladle chili into individual serving bowls. Sprinkle 1 tablespoon Cheddar cheese over each serving. Yield: 8 (1½-cup) servings.

PER SERVING: 195 CALORIES (16% FROM FAT)
FAT 3.5G (SATURATED FAT 1.2G)
PROTEIN 10.2G CARBOHYDRATE 33.5G
CHOLESTEROL 5MG   SODIUM 456MG

Coward's Chili

This chili is for all of you who prefer mild rather than wild flavor when it comes to heat.

1½ pounds ground round
2 cups chopped green pepper
2 cups coarsely chopped yellow onion
2 teaspoons chili powder
½ teaspoon ground cumin
1 cup water
½ teaspoon salt
¼ teaspoon freshly ground pepper
2 (15-ounce) cans kidney beans, drained
2 (14½-ounce) cans no-salt-added tomatoes, undrained and chopped
2 (8-ounce) cans no-salt-added tomato sauce
1 (6-ounce) can no-salt-added tomato paste

Cook ground round, green pepper, and onion in a Dutch oven over medium-high heat until beef is browned, stirring until it crumbles. Drain beef mixture, and pat dry with paper towels. Wipe drippings from Dutch oven with a paper towel.

Return beef mixture to Dutch oven. Stir in chili powder and ground cumin. Cook, stirring constantly, 1 minute. Add water and remaining ingredients. Bring chili to a boil; cover, reduce heat, and simmer 2 hours, stirring occasionally. Yield: 11 (1-cup) servings.

PER SERVING: 210 CALORIES (18% FROM FAT)
FAT 4.2G (SATURATED FAT 1.4G)
PROTEIN 19.3G CARBOHYDRATE 24.7G
CHOLESTEROL 38MG SODIUM 304MG

White Chili with Fresh Tomatoes

1 (15-ounce) can Great Northern beans, drained
Vegetable cooking spray
½ cup chopped onion
2 cloves garlic, minced
¾ cup chopped cooked chicken breast
½ teaspoon dried oregano
½ teaspoon ground cumin
¼ teaspoon ground coriander
Dash of ground red pepper
Dash of ground cloves
1 (14¼-ounce) can no-salt-added chicken broth
1 (4.5-ounce) can chopped green chiles, undrained
¾ cup chopped tomato, divided
⅛ teaspoon salt

Place ½ cup beans in a small bowl; mash and set aside. Reserve remaining whole beans.

Coat a medium saucepan with cooking spray; place over medium-high heat until hot. Add onion and garlic; sauté until tender. Stir in mashed and whole beans, chicken, and next 7 ingredients. Bring to a boil; cover, reduce heat, and simmer 15 minutes. Stir in ½ cup tomato and salt; cover and simmer 3 additional minutes.

To serve, ladle chili into individual bowls, and top evenly with remaining ¼ cup tomato. Yield: 2 servings.

PER SERVING: 336 CALORIES (13% FROM FAT)
FAT 4.9G (SATURATED FAT 0.8G)
PROTEIN 32.8G CARBOHYDRATE 41.2G
CHOLESTEROL 48MG SODIUM 749MG

CHICKEN CHILI

Vegetable cooking spray
2 teaspoons vegetable oil
4 cups coarsely chopped onion
1½ cups chopped green pepper
4 cloves garlic, thinly sliced
1½ pounds skinned, boned chicken breast, cut into ¼-inch pieces
¼ cup chili powder
1 tablespoon ground cumin
2 teaspoons ground coriander
½ teaspoon salt
½ teaspoon ground red pepper
2 (14½-ounce) cans no-salt-added whole tomatoes, undrained and chopped
1 (12-ounce) can beer
1 (10½-ounce) can low-sodium chicken broth
1 (6-ounce) can tomato paste
1 bay leaf
2 (15-ounce) cans garbanzo beans, drained

Coat a large Dutch oven with cooking spray; add oil. Place over medium-high heat until hot. Add onion, green pepper, and garlic; sauté 5 minutes or until tender. Add chicken, and cook, stirring constantly, 2 minutes or until browned.

Add chili powder and next 4 ingredients; cook, stirring constantly, 1 minute. Add chopped tomatoes and next 4 ingredients; bring to a boil. Cover, reduce heat, and simmer 40 minutes, stirring occasionally. Add beans, and cook, uncovered, 20 minutes, stirring occasionally. Discard bay leaf. Yield: 12 (1-cup) servings.

PER SERVING: 217 CALORIES (15% FROM FAT)
FAT 3.7G (SATURATED FAT 0.6G)
PROTEIN 20.0G   CARBOHYDRATE 28.0G
CHOLESTEROL 33MG   SODIUM 287MG

CHUNKY TURKEY CHILI

Vegetable cooking spray
1½ cups (1-inch pieces) cut onion
1 cup (1-inch pieces) cut green pepper
2 tablespoons coarsely chopped jalapeño pepper
3 cloves garlic, minced
1 pound freshly ground raw turkey
½ cup frozen whole-kernel corn
2 tablespoons chili powder
¼ teaspoon ground red pepper
⅛ teaspoon ground cumin
¼ teaspoon salt
2 (14½-ounce) cans no-salt-added whole tomatoes, undrained and chopped
1 (16-ounce) can pinto beans, undrained

Coat a medium saucepan with cooking spray; place over medium heat until hot. Add onion and green pepper; sauté 1 minute. Add jalapeño pepper and garlic; sauté 3 minutes or until onion is tender.

Add turkey; cook 5 minutes or until turkey is browned, stirring until it crumbles. Stir in corn and remaining ingredients. Bring to a boil; reduce heat, and simmer, uncovered, 20 minutes or until thoroughly heated. Yield: 6 (1⅓-cup) servings.

PER SERVING: 229 CALORIES (14% FROM FAT)
FAT 3.6G (SATURATED FAT 0.8G)
PROTEIN 22.5G   CARBOHYDRATE 28.1G
CHOLESTEROL 49MG   SODIUM 511MG

Turkey Labels

Some forms of ground turkey are higher in fat than others; check labels before buying.
• Ground raw turkey breast contains white meat only (lowest in fat).
• Ground turkey meat is meat minus skin and fat (may contain dark meat).
• Ground turkey is meat including skin and fat naturally on the bird.

TURKEY PICADILLO CHILI

Picadillo is a traditional dish in many Spanish-speaking countries. Here turkey replaces the usual ground meat, and the raisins and cinnamon add a slightly sweet taste.

Vegetable cooking spray
1 pound freshly ground raw turkey breast
½ cup sliced green onions
1 (4.5-ounce) can chopped green chiles, undrained
1 clove garlic, minced
½ cup raisins
3 tablespoons slivered almonds
1 teaspoon chili powder
½ teaspoon ground cumin
½ teaspoon ground cinnamon
¼ teaspoon ground cloves
¼ teaspoon ground red pepper
¼ teaspoon black pepper
2 (8-ounce) cans no-salt-added tomato sauce
1 (14½-ounce) can no-salt-added whole tomatoes, undrained and chopped
8 pimiento-stuffed olives, halved

Coat a large saucepan with cooking spray, and place over medium-high heat until hot. Add turkey, and cook until browned, stirring until it crumbles.

Add green onions, chiles, and garlic; cook 3 minutes. Add raisins and remaining ingredients. Cover, reduce heat, and simmer 15 minutes. Yield: 6 (1-cup) servings.

PER SERVING: 199 CALORIES (21% FROM FAT)
FAT 4.6G (SATURATED FAT 0.9G)
PROTEIN 19.1G CARBOHYDRATE 21.3G
CHOLESTEROL 49MG SODIUM 493MG

TURKEY CHILI WITH CORNMEAL DUMPLINGS

Vegetable cooking spray
1 pound freshly ground raw turkey breast
3 cups water
1 cup chopped onion
1 cup chopped green pepper
2 tablespoons chili powder
1 teaspoon dried oregano
¼ teaspoon salt
¼ teaspoon coarsely ground pepper
2 (14½-ounce) cans no-salt-added whole tomatoes, undrained
1 (19-ounce) can red kidney beans, drained
1 (10-ounce) package frozen whole-kernel corn
1 (6-ounce) can no-salt-added tomato paste
⅔ cup all-purpose flour
⅔ cup stone-ground yellow cornmeal
2 teaspoons baking powder
¼ teaspoon salt
2 tablespoons margarine, cut into small pieces and chilled
2 tablespoons minced fresh parsley
⅔ cup skim milk

Coat a Dutch oven with cooking spray; place over medium heat until hot. Add turkey, and cook until browned, stirring until it crumbles. Drain turkey, and return to pan. Add water and next 10 ingredients; bring to a boil. Reduce heat, and simmer, uncovered, 30 minutes, stirring occasionally.

Combine flour and next 3 ingredients; cut in margarine with a pastry blended until mixture resembles coarse meal. Stir in parsley. Add milk; stir just until dry ingredients are moistened. Drop batter by tablespoonfuls into hot chili; simmer, uncovered, 10 minutes. Cover and cook 10 minutes or until dumplings are done. To serve, ladle 1½ cups chili into each individual bowl; top each with 2 dumplings. Yield: 6 servings.

PER SERVING: 435 CALORIES (15% FROM FAT)
FAT 7.4G (SATURATED FAT 1.6G)
PROTEIN 30.4G CARBOHYDRATE 64.9G
CHOLESTEROL 40MG SODIUM 472MG

Corn and Pepper Chowder

CORN AND PEPPER CHOWDER

Vegetable cooking spray
1 teaspoon olive oil
1 cup chopped onion
1 cup chopped sweet red pepper
1 tablespoon plus 2 teaspoons all-purpose flour
½ teaspoon ground cumin
2 cups water
1⅓ cups peeled, cubed red potato
1 teaspoon chicken-flavored bouillon granules
2 cups frozen whole-kernel corn, thawed
1 cup evaporated skimmed milk
2 tablespoons canned chopped green chiles
¼ teaspoon black pepper
⅛ teaspoon ground red pepper
Fresh cilantro sprigs (optional)

Coat a large Dutch oven with cooking spray; add oil. Place over medium-high heat until hot. Add onion and sweet red pepper; sauté until tender. Stir in flour and cumin; cook 1 minute. Add water, potato, and bouillon granules. Bring mixture to a boil, stirring frequently. Cover, reduce heat, and simmer 10 minutes or until potato is tender and liquid is thickened.

Add corn and next 4 ingredients to Dutch oven; cook over medium heat 5 minutes or until thoroughly heated.

To serve, ladle chowder into individual bowls. Garnish each serving with a fresh cilantro sprig, if desired. Yield: 5 (1-cup) servings.

PER SERVING: 173 CALORIES (10% FROM FAT)
FAT 1.9G (SATURATED FAT 0.3G)
PROTEIN 7.9G   CARBOHYDRATE 34.0G
CHOLESTEROL 2MG   SODIUM 252MG

WHITE BEAN AND FENNEL CHOWDER

Vegetable cooking spray
2 cups chopped onion
¼ pound chopped reduced-fat, low-salt ham
2 cloves garlic, minced
4 cups water
2½ cups peeled, chopped red potato (about 1 pound)
2 cups chopped fennel bulb (about ½ pound)
1½ cups chopped carrot
2 (16-ounce) cans navy beans, undrained
2 tablespoons all-purpose flour
1 cup 2% low-fat milk
¼ teaspoon freshly ground pepper

Coat a large Dutch oven with cooking spray; place over medium heat until hot. Add onion, ham, and garlic; sauté 5 minutes. Add water and next 3 ingredients; bring to a boil. Cover, reduce heat, and simmer 20 minutes or until vegetables are tender.

Place 4 cups potato mixture in container of an electric blender or food processor; cover and process until smooth. Add potato puree to mixture in pan; stir well. Drain beans, reserving ½ cup liquid. Add beans and reserved liquid to pan.

Place flour in a bowl. Gradually add milk to flour, stirring with a wire whisk until blended; add to chowder. Cook over medium heat, stirring constantly, 5 minutes or until thickened. Stir in pepper. Yield: 8 (1½-cup) servings.

PER SERVING: 238 CALORIES (8% FROM FAT)
FAT 2.1G (SATURATED FAT 0.8G)
PROTEIN 14.6G CARBOHYDRATE 42.0G
CHOLESTEROL 10MG SODIUM 646MG

SPRING CHOWDER

1 tablespoon margarine
4 cups thinly sliced Vidalia or other sweet onion
1 cup chopped carrot
1 cup sliced celery
1 cup chopped extra-lean ham
3 cups chopped red potato (about 1¼ pounds)
1 (10½-ounce) can low-salt chicken broth
¼ cup all-purpose flour
2 cups 2% low-fat milk
¼ cup chopped fresh sage
½ teaspoon salt
¼ to ½ teaspoon pepper
⅛ teaspoon ground nutmeg
½ cup dry white wine
Sage sprigs (optional)

Melt margarine in a large Dutch oven over medium-high heat. Add onion, carrot, celery, and ham; sauté 10 minutes. Add potato and broth; bring to a boil. Cover, reduce heat, and simmer 45 minutes or until potato is tender.

Place flour in a bowl. Gradually add milk, stirring with a whisk until blended. Add milk mixture, chopped sage, salt, pepper, and nutmeg to chowder; cook over medium-low heat 2 minutes. Add wine; cook 10 minutes or until thickened, stirring frequently. Garnish with sage, if desired. Yield: 8 (1-cup) servings.

PER SERVING: 179 CALORIES (21% FROM FAT)
FAT 4.2G (SATURATED FAT 1.5G)
PROTEIN 9.0G CARBOHYDRATE 27.1G
CHOLESTEROL 14MG SODIUM 444MG

Manhattan Fish Chowder

MANHATTAN FISH CHOWDER

1 tablespoon margarine
1 cup chopped onion
1 cup chopped carrot
½ cup chopped celery
3 cups peeled, diced red potato (about 1¼ pounds)
⅓ cup reduced-calorie chili sauce
2 tablespoons tomato paste
1 tablespoon Worcestershire sauce
¾ teaspoon dried thyme
½ teaspoon hot sauce
2 (14½-ounce) cans no-salt-added whole tomatoes, undrained and chopped
2 (8-ounce) bottles clam juice
2 bay leaves
2 pounds grouper or other white fish fillets, cut into 1-inch pieces
¼ cup chopped fresh parsley
Additional chopped fresh parsley (optional)

Melt margarine in a large Dutch oven over medium heat. Add onion, carrot, and celery; sauté 5 minutes. Add potato and next 8 ingredients; bring to a boil. Cover, reduce heat, and simmer 50 minutes or until potato is tender.

Add fish and ¼ cup parsley to chowder; cover and simmer 5 minutes or until fish flakes easily when tested with a fork. Discard bay leaves. Ladle into individual bowls, and sprinkle with additional parsley, if desired. Yield: 8 (1½-cup) servings.

PER SERVING: 210 CALORIES (12% FROM FAT)
FAT 2.8G (SATURATED FAT 0.6G)
PROTEIN 24.9G CARBOHYDRATE 21.2G
CHOLESTEROL 42MG SODIUM 259MG

SALMON CHOWDER

½ pound fresh green beans
2 cups peeled, cubed potato
1 cup chopped onion
3 cups water
½ cup clam juice
1 tablespoon minced fresh tarragon
1 teaspoon chicken-flavored bouillon granules
¼ teaspoon ground white pepper
⅛ teaspoon garlic powder
1 pound salmon fillets, cut into ¾-inch pieces
⅓ cup all-purpose flour
2 cups skim milk, divided
¾ to 1 teaspoon grated lemon rind

Wash green beans; trim ends, and remove strings. Cut beans into ¾-inch pieces. Combine beans, potato, and next 7 ingredients in a Dutch oven. Bring mixture to a boil; cover, reduce heat, and simmer 15 minutes. Add salmon; cover and cook 5 minutes.

Combine flour and ½ cup milk in a small bowl, stirring with a wire whisk until smooth. Gradually add flour mixture and remaining 1½ cups milk to salmon mixture. Cook, stirring constantly, 15 minutes or until mixture is slightly thickened. Remove mixture from heat, and stir in grated lemon rind. Yield: 9 (1-cup) servings.

PER SERVING: 154 CALORIES (19% FROM FAT)
FAT 3.3G (SATURATED FAT 0.7G)
PROTEIN 14.7G CARBOHYDRATE 16.0G
CHOLESTEROL 21MG SODIUM 175MG

Did You Know?

The word chowder comes from the French *chaudière*, a caldron used by fishermen to make fresh seafood stew. Although clam chowder is probably the most well known, any type of fish or shellfish can be used to make chowder. The term is also used for thick vegetable stews that usually contain potatoes.

New England Clam Chowder

NEW ENGLAND CLAM CHOWDER

2 (44-ounce) cans steamer clams in shells,
    undrained
Vegetable cooking spray
3 cups chopped onion
2 cups cubed red potato (about 1½ pounds)
1 cup diced celery
2 slices turkey bacon, chopped
2 cups water
½ teaspoon salt
½ teaspoon dried thyme
¼ teaspoon coarsely ground pepper
3 fresh parsley sprigs
1 bay leaf
3 tablespoons all-purpose flour
2 cups 2% low-fat milk

Drain clams, reserving 1 cup clam liquid. Remove clams from shells; discard shells. Slip black skin off foot of each clam, and discard. Set clams aside.

Coat a Dutch oven with cooking spray; place over medium-high heat until hot. Add onion and next 3 ingredients; sauté 7 minutes. Add reserved clam liquid, water, and next 5 ingredients; bring to a boil. Cover, reduce heat, and simmer 20 minutes or until potato is tender. Discard parsley and bay leaf.

Place flour in a bowl. Gradually add milk, blending with a whisk; add to pan. Cook over medium heat 10 minutes or until thickened, stirring frequently. Stir in clams; cook 2 minutes or until heated. Yield: 9 (1-cup) servings.

Note: Substitute 2 pounds fresh clams in shells and 1 (8-ounce) bottle clam juice for the 2 cans of steamer clams and 1 cup drained liquid, if desired.

PER SERVING: 130 CALORIES (21% FROM FAT)
FAT 3.1G (SATURATED FAT 1.1G)
PROTEIN 8.4G   CARBOHYDRATE 16.6G
CHOLESTEROL 21MG   SODIUM 398MG

OYSTER-CORN CHOWDER

2 (12-ounce) containers Standard oysters,
  undrained
¼ cup all-purpose flour
1 tablespoon margarine
½ cup chopped onion
⅓ cup chopped celery
⅓ cup chopped carrot
4 cups 2% low-fat milk
2 cups diced red potato
1 (16-ounce) package frozen whole-kernel corn
1 teaspoon salt
½ teaspoon hot sauce
⅛ teaspoon pepper
¼ cup plus 3 tablespoons chopped green onions

Drain oysters, reserving juice; set oysters aside.
Place flour in a small bowl. Gradually add oyster juice,
stirring with a wire whisk until blended; set aside.

Melt margarine in a Dutch oven over medium
heat. Add onion, celery, and carrot, and sauté 5
minutes. Add milk and diced potato; bring to a simmer. Cover and cook 10 minutes. Add corn; cover
and cook 5 minutes. Add oysters, oyster juice mixture, salt, hot sauce, and pepper; cook, uncovered,
6 minutes or until edges of oysters begin to curl.
Ladle into soup bowls, and top with green onions.
Yield: 7 (1½-cup) servings.

PER SERVING: 244 CALORIES (23% FROM FAT)
FAT 6.2G (SATURATED FAT 2.5G)
PROTEIN 13.1G CARBOHYDRATE 36.1G
CHOLESTEROL 49MG SODIUM 517MG

SCALLOP CHOWDER

*If bay scallops are not available, you may substitute
larger sea scallops. Just cut the sea scallops into
fourths before adding to the chowder mixture.*

1 tablespoon margarine
1 cup chopped onion
½ cup diced celery
⅓ cup diced sweet red pepper
1 clove garlic, minced
¼ cup all-purpose flour
1½ cups diced red potato
1 cup frozen whole-kernel corn
½ cup water
¼ teaspoon salt
¼ teaspoon dried thyme
⅛ teaspoon pepper
3 (8-ounce) bottles clam juice
1 pound bay scallops
¼ cup chopped fresh parsley

Melt margarine in a Dutch oven over medium
heat. Add onion, celery, red pepper, and garlic;
sauté 8 minutes or until tender. Sprinkle onion
mixture with flour; stir well. Cook, stirring constantly, 1 minute. Add potato and next 6 ingredients; stir well. Bring to a boil; cover, reduce heat,
and simmer 20 minutes or until potato is tender.

Add scallops; cover and cook 4 minutes or until
scallops are opaque. Sprinkle with parsley. Yield: 7
(1-cup) servings.

PER SERVING: 150 CALORIES (14% FROM FAT)
FAT 2.3G (SATURATED FAT 0.4G)
PROTEIN 13.5G CARBOHYDRATE 19.4G
CHOLESTEROL 21MG SODIUM 428MG

Oyster-Corn Chowder

CARIBBEAN SHRIMP AND PUMPKIN CHOWDER

Madras curry powder, which is hotter than regular curry powder, can be found in the spice section of your supermarket.

1½ pounds unpeeled medium-size fresh
    shrimp
2 tablespoons vegetable oil
4 cups chopped onion
2 tablespoons Madras curry powder
1 tablespoon peeled, minced gingerroot
¼ teaspoon dried crushed red pepper
3 cloves garlic, crushed
5 cups clam juice
1 cup diced sweet red pepper
1 cup diced sweet yellow pepper
½ teaspoon salt
2 (14½-ounce) cans no-salt-added whole
    tomatoes, undrained and chopped
1 (6-ounce) can tomato paste
2 cups cubed, cooked fresh pumpkin
1 cup evaporated skimmed milk
⅓ cup minced green onions
¼ cup minced fresh parsley
2 tablespoons minced fresh cilantro
2 tablespoons lime juice

Peel and devein shrimp; set aside.

Heat oil in a large Dutch oven over medium heat. Add onion; sauté 7 minutes or until tender. Add curry powder, gingerroot, crushed red pepper, and garlic; sauté 2 minutes. Add clam juice and next 5 ingredients; bring to a boil. Cover, reduce heat, and simmer 20 minutes.

Add shrimp; cook, uncovered, 5 minutes or until shrimp turn pink. Stir in pumpkin and remaining ingredients; cook 5 minutes or until thoroughly heated. Yield: 16 (1-cup) servings.

PER SERVING: 123 CALORIES (21% FROM FAT)
FAT 2.9G (SATURATED FAT 0.5G)
PROTEIN 12.0G CARBOHYDRATE 13.3G
CHOLESTEROL 65MG SODIUM 333MG

CAJUN SEAFOOD AND SAUSAGE GUMBO

Not a fan of oysters? You can still make and enjoy gumbo. Just omit the oysters in this and other gumbos, if you prefer.

⅓ cup all-purpose flour
1 (12-ounce) container fresh Standard oysters,
    undrained
Vegetable cooking spray
2 cups frozen cut okra
2 cups chopped onion
1½ cups diced green pepper
1½ cups diced celery
2 cloves garlic, crushed
½ pound smoked turkey sausage, cut into
    ¼-inch slices
⅔ cup water
¼ cup chopped fresh parsley
2½ teaspoons paprika
¾ teaspoon dried thyme
½ teaspoon dried oregano
½ teaspoon ground white pepper
½ teaspoon ground red pepper
½ teaspoon black pepper
¼ teaspoon salt
2 (8-ounce) bottles clam juice
1 (14½-ounce) can no-salt-added whole
    tomatoes, undrained and chopped
1 (14¼-ounce) can no-salt-added chicken
    broth
2 small bay leaves
1 pound unpeeled small fresh shrimp
½ pound fresh lump crabmeat, drained
6 cups cooked long-grain rice (cooked without
    salt or fat)

Place ⅓ cup flour in a shallow baking pan. Bake at 350° for 1 hour or until very brown, stirring every 15 minutes. Set browned flour aside.

Drain oysters, reserving liquid; set liquid aside, and refrigerate oysters.

Coat a large Dutch oven with cooking spray; place over medium heat until hot. Add okra, chopped onion, green pepper, celery, and crushed garlic; cook 12 minutes or until tender, stirring frequently.

Cajun Seafood and Sausage Gumbo

Stir in browned flour. Add reserved oyster liquid, sausage, and next 13 ingredients; bring to a boil, stirring constantly. Reduce heat, and simmer, uncovered, 1 hour.

Peel and devein shrimp. Add shrimp, oysters, and crabmeat to pan; stir well. Cover and simmer 10 minutes or until shrimp turn pink and edges of oysters begin to curl. Discard bay leaves. Ladle ½ cup rice and 1 cup gumbo into each individual bowl. Yield: 12 servings.

PER SERVING: 272 CALORIES (16% FROM FAT)
FAT 4.9G (SATURATED FAT 1.2G)
PROTEIN 20.1G CARBOHYDRATE 36.4G
CHOLESTEROL 93MG SODIUM 431MG

Low-Fat Roux

Roux, made from slowly cooked flour and fat, is the typical thickener in gumbo. But you can brown flour in the oven without the fat. The longer it bakes, the more flavorful it becomes.

As the flour bakes, its color changes from white to blonde to golden to dark brown. This browned flour thickens the gumbo and adds a nutty, rich flavor.

LOUISIANA TURKEY-SEAFOOD GUMBO

(pictured on page 122)

¼ cup all-purpose flour
1 cup chopped green pepper
1¾ cups chopped celery
1½ cups chopped onion
2 cups water, divided
1¾ teaspoons chicken-flavored bouillon
   granules
2 (14½-ounce) cans no-salt-added whole
   tomatoes, undrained and chopped
3½ cups no-salt-added tomato juice
1 pound okra, sliced
3 cups chopped cooked turkey breast
3 tablespoons chopped fresh parsley
½ teaspoon garlic powder
½ teaspoon hot sauce
¼ teaspoon freshly ground black pepper
¼ teaspoon ground red pepper
¼ teaspoon dried thyme
1 bay leaf
1½ pounds unpeeled medium-size fresh
   shrimp
1 (12-ounce) container Standard oysters,
   drained

Place flour in a shallow baking pan. Bake at 400° for 12 to 14 minutes or until browned, stirring every 4 minutes. Set aside.

Combine green pepper, celery, onion, ⅓ cup water, and bouillon granules in a large Dutch oven. Cook over medium heat 10 to 12 minutes or until vegetables are tender. Stir in browned flour. Gradually stir in remaining 1⅔ cups water, tomatoes, and next 10 ingredients. Cover, reduce heat, and simmer 45 minutes.

Peel and devein shrimp. Add shrimp and oysters to pan; simmer 10 minutes or until shrimp turn pink and edges of oysters begin to curl. Discard bay leaf. Yield: 8 (2-cup) servings.

PER SERVING: 253 CALORIES (14% FROM FAT)
FAT 4.0G (SATURATED FAT 1.0G)
PROTEIN 32.6G CARBOHYDRATE 21.9G
CHOLESTEROL 150MG SODIUM 404MG

BEEF AND VEGETABLE RAGOÛT

1 (2-pound) beef brisket
Vegetable cooking spray
1½ cups water
1 teaspoon beef-flavored bouillon granules
½ teaspoon pepper
¼ teaspoon salt
2 cloves garlic, minced
1 (12-ounce) bottle beer
1½ pounds carrots, cut into ½-inch slices
½ pound unpeeled red potatoes, cut into
   ½-inch cubes
4 cups thinly sliced leeks (about 2 medium)
2 cups halved fresh mushrooms

Trim fat from brisket, and cut brisket into 1-inch cubes.

Coat a large Dutch oven with cooking spray, and place over medium-high heat until hot. Add brisket, and sauté 4 minutes or until browned. Drain brisket well; wipe drippings from pan with a paper towel.

Return brisket to pan. Add water and next 5 ingredients, and bring to a boil. Cover, reduce heat, and simmer 1 hour. Add carrot and potato; cover and simmer 2 hours. Add leeks and mushrooms; cover and simmer 30 minutes or until beef is very tender. Yield: 6 (1½-cup) servings.

PER SERVING: 351 CALORIES (33% FROM FAT)
FAT 12.8G (SATURATED FAT 4.5G)
PROTEIN 31.0G CARBOHYDRATE 27.8G
CHOLESTEROL 88MG SODIUM 379MG

Beef and Vegetable Ragoût

KENTUCKY BURGOO

1 pound lean boneless chuck steak
1½ teaspoons vegetable oil
8 cups canned no-salt-added beef broth,
    undiluted
1 pound skinned, boned chicken thighs
4 cups peeled, cubed baking potato
2½ cups chopped carrot
1 cup chopped celery
1 cup chopped onion
1½ teaspoons curry powder
1 teaspoon dried thyme
½ teaspoon salt
1 (14½-ounce) can whole tomatoes, undrained
    and coarsely chopped
1 clove garlic, minced
2 cups frozen whole-kernel corn, thawed
1 (10-ounce) package frozen lima beans,
    thawed

Trim fat from steak, and cut steak into 1-inch cubes. Heat vegetable oil in a large Dutch oven; add steak, and cook until browned on all sides. Add broth, and bring to a boil. Cover, reduce heat, and simmer 1 hour.

Trim excess fat from chicken thighs, and cut chicken into 1-inch cubes. Add chicken, potato, and next 8 ingredients to steak mixture; simmer, uncovered, 30 minutes or until vegetables are tender.

Add corn and lima beans to steak mixture; cook 15 minutes or until beans are tender. Yield: 10 (1½-cup) servings.

PER SERVING: 257 CALORIES (20% FROM FAT)
FAT 5.7G (SATURATED FAT 1.8G)
PROTEIN 18.2G CARBOHYDRATE 32.4G
CHOLESTEROL 24MG SODIUM 308MG

Kentucky Burgoo

INDEX

METRIC EQUIVALENTS

Metric Equivalents for Different Types of Ingredients

A standard cup measure of a dry or solid ingredient will vary in weight depending on the type of ingredient. A standard cup of liquid is the same volume for any type of liquid. Use the following chart when converting standard cup measures to grams (weight) or milliliters (volume).

Standard Cup	Fine Powder (ex. flour)	Grain (ex. rice)	Granular (ex. sugar)	Liquid Solids (ex. butter)	Liquid (ex. milk)
1	140 g	150 g	190 g	200 g	240 ml
¾	105 g	113 g	143 g	150 g	180 ml
⅔	93 g	100 g	125 g	133 g	160 ml
½	70 g	75 g	95 g	100 g	120 ml
⅓	47 g	50 g	63 g	67 g	80 ml
¼	35 g	38 g	48 g	50 g	60 ml
⅛	18 g	19 g	24 g	25 g	30 ml

Useful Equivalents for Liquid Ingredients by Volume

¼ tsp					=	1 ml	
½ tsp					=	2 ml	
1 tsp					=	5 ml	
3 tsp	=	1 tbls		=	½ fl oz	=	15 ml	
		2 tbls	=	⅛ cup	=	1 fl oz	=	30 ml
		4 tbls	=	¼ cup	=	2 fl oz	=	60 ml
		5⅓ tbls	=	⅓ cup	=	3 fl oz	=	80 ml
		8 tbls	=	½ cup	=	4 fl oz	=	120 ml
		10⅔ tbls	=	⅔ cup	=	5 fl oz	=	160 ml
		12 tbls	=	¾ cup	=	6 fl oz	=	180 ml
		16 tbls	=	1 cup	=	8 fl oz	=	240 ml
		1 pt	=	2 cups	=	16 fl oz	=	480 ml
		1 qt	=	4 cups	=	32 fl oz	=	960 ml
					33 fl oz	=	1000 ml	=	1 l

Useful Equivalents for Dry Ingredients by Weight

(To convert ounces to grams, multiply the number of ounces by 30.)

1 oz	=	1/16 lb	=	30 g
4 oz	=	¼ lb	=	120 g
8 oz	=	½ lb	=	240 g
12 oz	=	¾ lb	=	360 g
16 oz	=	1 lb	=	480 g

Useful Equivalents for Cooking/Oven Temperatures

	Fahrenheit	Celcius	Gas Mark
Freeze Water	32° F	0° C	
Room Temperature	68° F	20° C	
Boil Water	212° F	100° C	
Bake	325° F	160° C	3
	350° F	180° C	4
	375° F	190° C	5
	400° F	200° C	6
	425° F	220° C	7
	450° F	230° C	8
Broil			Grill

Useful Equivalents for Length

(To convert inches to centimeters, multiply the number of inches by 2.5.)

1 in					=	2.5 cm		
6 in	=	½ ft			=	15 cm		
12 in	=	1 ft			=	30 cm		
36 in	=	3 ft	=	1 yd	=	90 cm		
40 in					=	100 cm	=	1 m